TEACHING, LEARNING,
AND THE MIND

TEACHING, LEARNING, AND THE MIND

YOUNG PAI

UNIVERSITY OF MISSOURI
KANSAS CITY

Houghton Mifflin Company • **Boston**
Atlanta
Dallas
Geneva, Illinois
Hopewell, New Jersey
Palo Alto

Printed in the U.S.A.

Library of Congress Catalog Card Number: 72–3512

ISBN: 0–395–12663–0

Excerpts reprinted by permission of the publisher from John Dewey: *How We Think* (Lexington, Mass.: D. C. Heath and Company, 1933).

Excerpts reprinted by permision of the publisher from John Dewey: *Democracy and Education.* Copyright 1916 by The Macmillan Company, twenty-fifth printing 1952.

Excerpts from the book *A Treatise of Human Nature* by David Hume, intro. by A. D. Lindsay, Everyman's Library Edition, published by E. P. Dutton & Co., Inc. and used with their permission and that of J. M. Dent & Sons Ltd.

Figures from "Field Theory of Learning" by Kurt Lewin (Yearbook of the National Society for the Study of Education, 1942, Vol. II) used by permission of publisher.

Excerpts from *The Concept of Mind* (1949) by Gilbert Ryle reprinted by permission of Barnes & Noble, the Hutchinson University Library, and the author.

Excerpts from *Cumulative Record*, Enlarged Edition, B. F. Skinner. Copyright ‹ 1959, 1961. Reprinted by permission of Appleton-Century-Crofts, Educational Division, Meredith Corporation.

Excerpts from *Science and Human Behavior* by B. F. Skinner reprinted by permission of the publisher. Copyright ‹ 1953 by The Macmillan Company, sixth printing April 1968.

Excerpts from *The Technology of Teaching*, B. F. Skinner. Copyright ‹ 1968. Reprinted by permission of Appleton-Century-Crofts, Educational Division, Meredith Corporation.

Excerpts from *Text-Book of Psychology* by E. B. Titchener reprinted by permission.

FOR
JEANNETTE, DAVID, AND LORAINE

Contents

EDITOR'S PREFACE

What is this mystery, this "thing," this entity called The Human Mind? Is it, as Gilbert Ryle cracked, "The ghost in the machine?" Or, in this age of electronic simulation, is it the machine itself?

Time was when the mind was thought to be a finite set of faculties—"mental muscles"—which, like the muscles in the body, were given at birth and awaited exercise and strengthening for use at maturity. Education is the name given to the long program of intellectual calisthenics necessary to bring those "muscles" to full power. One.

Then, the mind was conceived as an "organizing box," a receiving and sorting station where the chaotic fragments of ordinary perception are gathered in, filed in orderly fashion, and kept in storage for later use. Education is the name given to the systematic storing process in which the teacher pre-organizes the fragments into a curriculum before putting them into the mind. Two.

Later, the word *mind* was brushed off as merely a "metaphor," a name we made up to "explain" behavior. The metaphor is not important. The behavior *is*. Behavior is controlled, i.e., maintained or extinguished, by reinforcement. Education is the name given to the orchestration of positive and negative reinforcements (rewards and punishments) designed to establish good and delete bad behavior. Three.

Then, the human mind was redefined once more. It was not a metaphor, but a "class" name for a certain mode of behavior, namely, that behavior which exhibits purpose and in which experience is gradually reconstructed into more humane and manageable form. Education is the name given to that process in which the individual is taught reflective thinking and the art of "reconstructing experience" through solving problems. Four.

Finally, the human mind may or may not be all of the above.

But there is an uneasy feeling that something vital, possibly unnameable, has been left out. Mind must work with *meaning*. Through some unknown and undetected avenue, meaning must somehow emerge in the individual before mind can exhibit activity, before the individual can determine what is, literally, worth "putting his mind to." In this phenomenological understanding of "mind," education is the name given to that encounter with experience in which the person becomes increasingly aware of those meanings in his life to which thought, reflection, and purposeful activity are to be directed. Five.

Well, there are others. But these five theories of teaching, learning, and mind are central to an understanding of American education today. In this volume, Professor Pai has put together a well articulated, clearly explained, and eminently readable account of these five theories and how they function in today's schools.

For all of the thought and concern and scholarship given to it, education continues to be the most complicated, the most mysterious, the most baffling of human undertakings. In the United States today we desperately search for a mode of instruction which will make the lives of our young both rewarding and humane, both self-satisfying and giving. A careful study of the five theories examined in this book will show how far, or not so far, we have all come in trying to unravel this puzzle.

The book is a textbook, meant to be learned from and taught from. As such, it is designed for courses in the philosophical and psychological foundations of education. Too often, these approaches have been made disparate and unconnected; here, Professor Pai brings them fruitfully back together again. We see how the philosopher's concern with *Man* sooner or later must find expression in the concrete behavior of the psychologists' subjects, individual *men*.

For teachers in training, for the experienced teacher in the classroom, for the school administrator, and for the interested

and concerned parent, this volume provides a working knowledge of the major theories by which boys and girls "go to
school" in the 1970's.

Van Cleve Morris
Dean, College of Education
University of Illinois at Chicago Circle

PREFACE

This book grew out of my class in social-philosophical foundations of education, where we attempted to examine critically certain theoretical and philosophical bases of various educational concepts, "theories," and practices for the purpose of helping prospective teachers develop a sound basis for evaluating disparate claims and proposals in education. The relationship between teaching and learning theories and concepts of man's mind is complex and their implications are many. Hence, not only can we say many more things about the topics discussed herein but we need to study them more thoroughly. However, since this book is written primarily for those who have not had much work in philosophy of education our discussion had to remain on a fairly elementary level. But those who are more advanced in their studies can benefit from doing further reading in the sources indicated at the end of each chapter.

While writing this book I have incurred many debts. Professor Van Cleve Morris has given me many useful suggestions all through this project. To Professors Bruce Baker and Martin Levit go many thanks for their reactions and comments during the planning stages of this book. In fact, it was at Professor Levit's suggestion that I decided to add a brief section on phenomenology and education. Lastly, it would have taken many more months to complete the final draft of the manuscript without the efficient and competent help of Miss Anna Borserine and Mrs. Dawna Holmes, who typed the original draft and its revision respectively. To Joyce Bolander, David Jensen, and Clarence Hughes, our graduate assistants, go my sincere appreciation for doing much of the proofreading chores and also giving me some invaluable criticisms from the student's point of view. Finally, for their support and understanding I am most grateful to my wife and children, who have been inconvenienced and neglected by my preoccupation with this book.

Young Pai
University of Missouri–Kansas City

1

Introduction

Today there is a great variety of diverging opinions regarding education, but the centrality of teaching in the educative process is not disputed, nor is there serious argument about the need to look for a more valid, reliable, and adequate approach to teaching. Any attempt at developing such methods and theories of teaching must be founded on a critical evaluation of existing views and a sound understanding of the nature of learning and the mind. As Boyd Bode once observed:

> How we teach is conditioned by what we assume the nature of learning to be. . . . As soon as we undertake to create a special environment, in the form of a school for the special purpose of promoting learning, we become involved in the question of what learning is. Our conception of learning has a direct bearing on method. It also has a bearing on educational aims or objectives because the question of what learning is can be answered only in terms of what the mind is; and our conception of the mind, in turn, will decide what we consider to be "good" for the mind, in terms of an educational program.[1]

Accordingly, the central concern of this book is to examine critically certain theories of learning and concepts of the mind as the psychological and philosophical bases of five major teaching theories, viz., the formal discipline, apperceptive, behavioristic, cognitive, and phenomenological theories. I chose these particular theories because of the impact they have on today's educational beliefs and practices. While very few, if any, serious-minded educators advocate the formal discipline and apperceptive theories any more, certain aspects of these views are still subsumed in many of our educational procedures and arguments. The central themes of these

1. Boyd Henry Bode, *How We Learn*, p. 6.

theories are reflected in such practical measures as the drills and recitations in our classrooms, the exclusive emphasis on the logical rules for correct thinking, the teaching of foreign languages as a means of disciplining the learner's mind, and the formalized steps employed in introducing new subject matter. Of course, these educational practices can be supported on other grounds. Historically they have most often been defended and justified in terms of the basic premises of the formal discipline and apperceptive theories of teaching. Furthermore, the criticisms of contemporary schools made by such well-known educators as Robert M. Hutchins, Mortimer J. Adler, and Arthur E. Bester concur with the general philosophical orientations of these theories, which, though dead as working theories, continue to affect many teachers.

As to the behavioristic, cognitive, and phenomenological theories of teaching and learning, whether we agree or disagree with any of these points of view, the fact of their impact on today's education is beyond dispute. Programmed learning and teaching machines are only two examples of the direct impingement of behaviorism on the technology of teaching. Our increasing concern with the learner's interest, freedom, motivation, insight, and discovery indicates the growing influence of the cognitive and phenomenological views. In short, today we can discern at least three different major trends in education. Because these outlooks, old and new, continue to have practical consequences in our educational endeavor, it behooves us to examine the foundations upon which they rest. My primary interest here is not to point out the "best" theory of teaching but to analyze these major views of teaching and their underlying premises as a basis for the development of a more consistent, rationally justifiable, and empirically sound theory of teaching. In the following pages I shall briefly discuss the need for this type of study as an important part of teachers' education.

With rapid growth in the field of education and other cognate disciplines we are likely to see a corresponding increase in the number of teaching theories representing disparate psychological and philosophical perspectives. These theories, in turn, are introduced to prospective teachers as an essential part of their professional training, but too often without a critical study of their theoretical foundations. As a result the "average" teacher tends to adopt certain features of different theories of teaching which frequently contradict and conflict with each other. And as new theories are added to the existing views the teacher becomes more confused and muddled about his own approaches to teaching and learning. Consequently, he is more likely to follow a set of "blind" routines as his method of teaching, or he is tempted to conform to some traditionally established ways of teaching. These routines, while applicable to a very specific and narrow range of teaching-learning situations, become fragmented and inflexible because they lack a theoretical framework. Many routine-oriented teachers attempt to deal with changes in their classroom situations by continuing to follow the method to which they have become blindly accustomed, while others adopt a different and new, but equally disconnected, set of routines. Some resort to a trial-and-error approach. Teachers who lack theoretical perspective tend to be too rigid and fragmented to cope successfully with change and novel circumstances. Not infrequently the expression "experienced teacher" stands for someone who has a large repertoire of routines rather than for a person who has progressively grown in understanding of the teaching-learning processes through his inquiries and teaching experience. What will help a teacher to deal effectively with new demands is not mere routines and gimmicks, but a theoretical and philosophical perspective from which he can develop appropriate means of dealing with change and evaluating newly acquired knowledge about the process of education.

As the breadth and depth of our knowledge about human behavior, society and its institutions, and the politico-economic variables which affect them grows and becomes more sophisticated, we see a similar rise in the number of disparate views in regard to school organization, teaching, curriculum, school financing, etc. The new opinions are so numerous today that the teacher can no longer rely on his immediate personal experience or tradition and common sense to evaluate these diverging claims. This then suggests that the teacher must have not only a more comprehensive understanding of such cognate disciplines as psychology, sociology, anthropology, history, and philosophy but also a set of criteria by which claims and assertions can be scrutinized for their validity and adequacy. In R. S. Peters' words:

> ... [Educational] procedures are constantly under discussion and vary according to different people's conceptions of the subjects which they are teaching; fundamental questions concerned with principles underlying school organization, class management and the curriculum are constantly being raised; and in the area of moral education the task is made more perplexing by the variations of standards which characterize a highly differentiated society. The question therefore is not whether a modern teacher indulges in philosophical reflection about what he is doing; it is rather whether he does it in a sloppy or in a rigorous manner.[2]

Clearly, the teacher must reflect critically and rigorously about what he is doing and his reasons for doing it. But apart from the teacher's need for personal clarity concerning education and his tasks related to it, there is yet another reason why the teacher should inquire about the grounds of his educational beliefs and practices.

In recent years the public has become much more acutely aware of the social functions of the school, it has become increasingly concerned with the failure of the school as a specialized social institution in meeting our individual as well as societal needs. Consequently, education is seen not only as a means of solving our social, economic, and moral problems, but its breakdown is thought to be a contributing causal factor in many of today's maladies. For example, rising juvenile

2. R. S. Peters, "The Philosophy of Education," *The Study of Education*, J. W. Tibble, ed., pp. 81–82.

delinquency, increased use of drugs by students of practically all ages, chaotic conditions in inner city schools, and allegedly growing sexual promiscuity have all been cited as only a few of the many consequences of having ineffective and outdated educational policies and procedures. In other words, our social and moral problems are said to be the products of a sick society and a dysfunctional system of education. For these and other reasons which we need not go into here, the public is becoming less willing to leave the matters of curriculum, teaching method, and even school organization and administration in the hands of teachers and administrators. Under these circumstances it is not enough that administrators are efficient in their offices and teachers are effective in their classrooms, for they must also be able to "defend [their] opinions in an informed and intelligent way so that [they] can hold [their] own in the welter of public discussion [and scrutiny]. The simple truth, in other words, is that the teacher has to learn to think for himself about what he is doing. He can no longer rely on an established tradition."[3] In a society where the quality of education provided by the school depends heavily on the financial support and moral approval of the public, the educator's ability to explain and to defend his educational policies and practices in an informed and persuasive way is imperative as a means of winning the public's vote of confidence and hence its support. To say that the teacher must think for himself is to say that he should be able to determine the validity and adequacy of educational beliefs and practices by detecting and correcting conceptual blunders and ambiguities, logical inconsistencies, and hidden but unwarranted assumptions found therein. Only through this kind of philosophical inquiry can the teacher hope to develop consistent, coherent, and socially relevant beliefs about the ends and means of education and also be able to justify his stand to the concerned public.

In the preceding pages I have tried to show briefly the

---

3. *Ibid.*, p. 82.

importance of and the need to philosophize about education. But why must we be concerned with teaching theories, particularly when psychology already has a considerable fund of reliable knowledge about learning, growth and development, and perception? What connection is there between concepts of the mind and theories of teaching and learning? Let us first look at the relationship between teaching and learning theories before we examine the ways in which philosophical concepts of the mind are relevant to a discussion of teaching and learning.

The most apparent distinction we can make between teaching and learning theories is that we may think of the former as largely prescriptive while regarding the latter as basically descriptive in nature. Teaching theories, as we know today, are mostly prescriptive in that they make explicit "recommendations" about how we can teach more effectively. In other words, a teaching theory is concerned with what we "ought" to do to promote and facilitate certain kinds of learning. Therefore, it contains not only empirical data on learning and other variables which affect it, but it also includes practical statements concerning what we should or should not do. These practical statements may be social, moral, or even political. The suggestions as to how teaching ought to be conducted are explicitly or implicitly bound up with our beliefs about what is worth teaching. Therefore, teaching theories can often provide us with the criteria by which instruction can be criticized and evaluated. In short, these theories are largely normative in nature and function.

Unlike theories of teaching, learning theories are descriptive in nature. That is, a learning theory is a system of empirical propositions or laws which are connected to each other by terms or constructs which do not necessarily involve directly and immediately observable referents (with the possible exception of B. F. Skinner's radical behaviorism). The primary function of a learning theory is to explain or describe how learning occurs. Hence, a valid theory of learning should not only increase our power to predict and control future events but it should also give us a consistent and coherent body of explanations as a basis for further understanding of the phenomena under investigation. Learning theories describe the circumstances under which learning does occur but do not imply what, how, or even whether we ought to teach. This indicates that teaching is only one of many situations under which learning can take place. In point of fact, children can and do learn without teaching in any deliberate and educational sense. Even under the most competent teaching there can be no guarantee that any learning will actually transpire, for the occurence of learning depends as much on the variables related to the learner himself and to other environmental factors as on teaching. However, this does not mean that learning theories are irrelevant in developing teaching theories, because "it is largely from a theory of learning that we can develop defensible notions of how crucial factors in the learning-teaching situations can be most effectively manipulated."[4]

A theory of teaching should be based on a sound theory of learning, because it "is concerned with how what one wishes to teach can best be learned, with improving rather than describing learning."[5] Unlike learning theories, teaching theories are not merely concerned with acquiring knowledge about teaching, but they help determine what we should do to promote the kind of learning we regard as educationally desirable. A practical theory like a teaching theory is not the end product of the pursuit of knowledge, but it is constructed to guide us in deciding the manner in which we are to teach.[6] Thus, the soundness of a teaching theory should be assessed on the basis of the validity of its empirical and theoretical elements as well as the ability of its prescriptive statements, or recommendations, to help us achieve those instructional objectives we have in view.

4. David P. Ausubel, *Educational Psychology*, p. 13.
5. Jerome Bruner, *Toward a Theory of Instruction*, p. 40.
6. Paul H. Hirst, "Educational Theory," *The Study of Education,* J. W. Tibble, ed., p. 40.

In addition to the prescriptive-descriptive distinction we have discussed is the fundamental distinction that teaching theories, as set forth today, are collections of explicit suggestions for achieving effective teaching, while learning theories belong to more systematic and comprehensive theories of human behavior. A teaching theory as a set of recommendations may or may not be based on psychological, sociocultural, and philosophical premises about learning, human nature and development, and man's relationship with his society. A teaching theory is not an integral part of any systematic theory of human behavior nor does it necessarily imply a particular world view. But contrary to teaching theories, learning theories belong to larger and more systematic theories of human behavior, which rest on a number of implicit or explicit philosophical premises about man, the universe, and science. And though learning theories are descriptive in the way in which we have already discussed, it can be argued that, as part of a larger philosophical view of things, they contain prescriptive elements in the sense of "suggesting" how we should look at human behavior, as does any scientific theory. For example, Skinner's theory of learning is only a part of his larger theory of human behavior, which is founded on several assumptions about the nature of man, his world, and knowledge. Hence, Skinnerian behaviorism represents not only a psychological perspective but also an implicit world view, which is in part rooted in the belief that the only reliable source of human knowledge is that which can be directly observed. The Skinnerian theory of learning, though stated in terms that are publically verifiable, is tantamount to a "recommendation" that learning should be understood or interpreted according to Skinner's criteria of knowledge and science. In view of what has been said, we should not then regard teaching theories as theories in the same sense in which learning theories have been called theories.

Finally, as Bode pointed out earlier, our conceptions of the mind not only influence the ways in which we see teaching and learning but they "will decide what we consider to be 'good' for the mind, in terms of an educational program."[7] Though it is doubtful that specific aims of education can be deduced from any single concept of the mind without positing all sorts of premises about what is worthwhile for man and his relationship with the society and its manifold dimensions, our view of the mind does provide us with a basis for deciding what is to be taught and in what manner. For example, if we conceive the mind to be a metaphysical substance or an entity without any sensible qualities but possessing such mental powers as the power of logical thinking, the power of abstract thinking, and the power of imagination, we are likely to regard the cultivation of such mental capacities as desirable ends of education. Our empirical understanding of the learning process plus other practical concerns will determine the method by which these powers may be developed. In other words, the concepts of the mind we accept tell us something about the general nature of the being to be educated, trained, or indoctrinated. In addition, our notions of the mind and its nature are fundamentally connected with our world views. Not only do our concepts of learning and teaching tacitly presuppose certain concepts of the mind but they reflect the metaphysical and epistemological stands we take in regard to the nature of science, knowledge, and reality. To hold that the mind is a metaphysical substance is to suggest that the sources of our knowledge of reality are not limited to those experiences that can be publicly shared. On the other hand, to contend that the term *mind* is just another expression for certain complex neural processes and that the word *substance* is devoid of any cognitive, empirical meaning is to imply that intersubjective experiences are the only reliable source of our knowledge about matters of fact. And because learning theories do presuppose certain philosophical perspectives, these psychologies of learning can be criticized and evaluated by attacking or defending their premises about the mind and

7. Bode, *How We Learn*, p. 6.

what constitutes meaning, evidence, and truth. "The most effective way to become intelligent about the business of education, in both its narrower and its broader aspects, is to explore the problem of learning [and teaching] with reference to its implications regarding the nature of the mind."[8]

BIBLIOGRAPHY

Ausubel, David P., *Educational Psychology.* New York: Holt, Rinehart and Winston, Inc., 1968.

Bode, Boyd Henry, *How We Learn.* Boston: D. C. Heath and Company, 1940.

Bruner, Jerome, *Toward a Theory of Instruction.* Cambridge, Mass.: Harvard University Press, 1966.

Hirst, Paul H., "Educational Theory," *The Study of Education,* J. W. Tibble, ed. London: Routledge and Kegan Paul, 1966.

Peters, R. S., "The Philosophy of Education," *The Study of Education,* J. W. Tibble, ed. London: Routledge and Kegan Paul, 1966.

8. *Ibid.,* "Preface.

2

The Formal Discipline Theory, Faculty Psychology, and the Substantive View of Mind

THE FORMAL DISCIPLINE THEORY OF TEACHING

The formal discipline theory of teaching is based on the belief that man has unique mental capacities or faculties* and that teaching should be seen as a process by which these powers are strengthened through a variety of appropriate exercises. That is, by having the learner use his faculties we develop and strengthen them, for "the power of the mind to put forth any kind of activity is developed by occasioning such activity."[1] In the late nineteenth century, J. B. Wickersham, State Superintendent of Public Instruction of Pennsylvania, pointed out:

> No means are known whereby the faculties of the mind can be developed but by exercising them. By the potent spell of the magic word Exercise, is evoked all human power. The proof of this proposition is found in multitudes of facts. The senses grow more acute by using them. The memory is improved by remembering, the reason by reasoning, the imagination by imagining. All these powers, too, become weak if not used. These facts may be learned from each person's own experience, or from observation upon others. The law inferred from them is fixed and universal.[2]

In other words, activity or exercise is the only effective means of developing the mental powers. Such a teaching principle as "the several mental powers can be developed only by occa-

---

*The terms *capacities, powers,* and *faculties* will be used interchangeably in this chapter.
1. Boyd Henry Bode, *How We Learn,* p. 85.
2. *Ibid.*

sioning their appropriate activity," can be inferred from our personal experiences and the observations of others. Perhaps it is this apparent congruence between the formal discipline theory and our personal experiences as well as "common sense" notions about the human mind that have enabled the theory to be so influential in education.

Historically, a wide range of faculties were attributed to the mind by the advocates of the formal discipline theory. Thomas Reid, a faculty psychologist, imputed eight powers to the mind, viz., the powers of external senses, memory, conception, analysis of complex objects and compounding of simple objects, judging, reasoning, tasting, and moral perception.[3] Noah Porter enumerated "the presentative, or observing faculty, the representative or creative faculty, the thinking or the generalizing faculty" as three leading faculties of the mind.[4] There were others who attributed a greater or a lesser number of powers to the mind, but in general the capacities of the mind were classified into the following six broad categories: the powers of perception, memory, imagination, reasoning, feeling, and willing. The first four were said to belong to the intellect, the last two to the soul or conscience. These powers, of course, do not develop all at once but in the general sequence in which they are listed. Since the proponents of the formal discipline theory believed that the curricular organization should relate to the developmental sequence of these powers, they emphasized the activities dealing with sense perception and memorization of facts in elementary and secondary schools. Studies of more abstract and rational subjects such as logic, philosophy, and rhetoric were assigned at college and university levels to develop the abstract and rational faculties of the mind as well as the "powers of the soul," namely, the powers of willing and making moral judgments. Though the advocates of the formal discipline theory regarded teaching as involving such direct

---

3. James Walker, ed., *Reid's Essays on Intellectual Powers of Man*, pp. 28–31.
4. Noah Porter, *The Human Intellect*, p. 77.

instructional procedures as drilling, memorizing, and reciting, they did not see teaching as a direct cause of learning but more as a means of facilitating and providing conditions under which learning could occur. Accordingly, Emerson E. White insisted that "the teacher is but the occasioner of right activity in the learner," for the actual training of the mental powers depends upon the learner's "self-exerted energy."[5] And therefore the most appropriate function of teaching was thought to be to stimulate this energy.[6] (It is interesting to note that most educators today believe that teaching does not automatically and necessarily lead to learning. This means that we can only arrange those conditions which are believed to be most conducive for the desired learning to occur. In short, teaching is only one of many variables which affect learning.)

Central to the formal discipline theory of teaching is the belief that mental powers are strengthened by exercise and frequent use. Once the faculties are trained, the effects endure and the developed powers can be called into operation on appropriate occasions. In White's words:

> Every normal act of the mind leaves as an enduring result an increased power to act and a tendency to act again in like manner. Power and tendency are the resultants of all mental action. The power and tendency of the mind to observe are increased by observing; to imagine by imagining; to judge by judging; to reason by reasoning, etc.[7]

This approach to teaching is indeed analogous to the training of muscles. That is, muscles are strengthened by exercise; it matters little whether the exercise is done by lifting bricks or weights specifically designed for such a purpose. Of course, special weights are more convenient to handle than bricks, but essentially both bricks and weights constitute materials with which muscles can be exercised. Similarly, transmission of

5. Emerson E. White, *The Art of Teaching*, p. 39.
6. *Ibid.*
7. *Ibid.*

subject matter was not the primary goal of teaching, the exercising of mental powers was. While, in general, subject matter was regarded as important only as materials with which to train the mind, some formal disciplinarians insisted that the nature of the materials did affect the learning process. Again, White points out:

> The several studies in a school course do not afford an equally valuable mental training, though all may afford a training, and a helpful training. The elementary studies, for example, do not equally train the power of observation, even when taught by an "observational method," nor is an observational method equally applicable to all elementary studies. No one study affords equally effective training in all directions, and certainly all studies do not give equally valuable training in any one direction. There is no ground for the claim that all studies have equal educational value, either as discipline or as knowledge. A course of school training should clearly include at least the elements of knowledge in all the fundamental branches. This is necessary for the acquisition of higher knowledge, as well as for the harmonious development of the mental powers.[8]

Contrary to the claims of some formal disciplinarians it would seem entirely reasonable to think that some materials are better suited for training certain kinds of powers than others. For example, logic, mathematics, and philosophy appear to be more appropriate in training the power of reasoning than in developing the power of perception. Since exercising the power of reasoning is nothing more than reasoning itself, any subject matter which is fundamentally rational would have more disciplinary power than nonrational subject matter. Since it is not possible to learn to think correctly without knowing the rules for correct thinking "there can be no effective training of the powers to know that does not give clear and definite knowledge."[9] So contends White. The fact that the acquisition of knowledge is unavoidable in the process of training mental capacities should not

8. *Ibid.*, p. 42.
9. *Ibid.*, p. 43.

suggest that imparting knowledge is the primary aim of teaching, for trained mental powers enable the learner to deal successfully with all sorts of problems and conflicts yet to be encountered. For example, we may forget the philosophical ideas we have learned but the power of reasoning developed through the study of philosophy will endure. We may use the trained rational capacity in dealing with nonphilosophical problems requiring logical reasoning. The power of observation developed through scientific studies can be used later to observe other life situations, and the faculty of memory strengthened through studying languages can be applied in remembering vital information relating to other, more practical affairs in life. Since the trained faculties endure even after we forget the content of what we learned, we must not be excessively concerned with learning subject matter.

> Mental power is not only more abiding than knowledge, but is of greater practical utility. While knowledge is a necessary guide in human effort, mental power gives acumen, grasp, strength, inspiration, and these are the winners of success in all the activities and conflicts of life. Even so called practical knowledge, to be of real utility for guidance, must be thought out and applied by an intelligent mind. . . .
>
> . . . I have elsewhere stated that if my mind were a tablet and with a sponge I should erase every fact learned in school and college, and not applied at the time in some art, I should not be intellectually very poor, but were I to lose the mental power gained in the mastery of these facts, so many of which were long since happily forgotten, I should be poor indeed. The abiding practical result of my school and college training, such as it was, is *soul power*. . . . It is thus seen that in education the act of acquiring knowledge is more important than the knowledge acquired. . . . Whatever knowledge is taught a child should be so taught that the act of acquiring it shall be of greater worth than the knowledge acquired. . . .
>
> No intelligent person questions the value of practical knowledge or the importance of properly including such knowledge in school courses, and certain few modern educators hold that the practical worth of knowledge in life lessens its value as a means

of mental discipline. The one result to be secured in teaching knowledge, whatever may be its nature, is the effective training of the power to acquire and express it. To this end it must be taught and acquired by methods that put the developing of power before knowledge.[10]

Today there are many educators who, on quite different grounds, warn us against narrowly practical education. That is, we should not be preoccupied with the immediate utility of what is learned at school, for excessively practical education leads to a heavily routine-oriented mode of living which, because routines apply only to a very narrow range of circumstances, is ineffective in dealing with change and novel situations. The routines that are immediately practical may in fact hinder the realization of an objective in the long run.

Transfer of Learning

One of the basic principles of the formal discipline theory is the notion that the transfer of learning occurs automatically as a result of strengthened mental powers. In other words, special forms of training such as studying Latin improve the general capacity of the mind, e.g., the ability to recall, because once the mental powers are developed they can be called into operation whenever appropriate situations occur. Returning again to the muscle analogy, once muscles are trained they can be used to lift books, bend wires, and move furniture. It matters little whether their training was accomplished with the equipment specifically made for this purpose or by utilizing commonplace objects. What matters is that the muscles have been strengthened through appropriate exercises and the trained muscles can be used to do a wide variety of tasks. In short, the formal disciplinarians see transfer of learning as occurring automatically. They point out that the more we exercise our faculties the more they develop, and the more they develop the greater will be the transfer of

10. *Ibid.*, pp. 43–45.

learning. Pedagogically this means that the learner's interest in a given task is unimportant, for the most effective learning occurs through drills, memorization, and recitations. Although these teaching procedures do not necessarily follow from the formal discipline theory, many educators believed them to be the most appropriate means of disciplining the mind. By now it should not be difficult to understand why for so long, teachers have been seen as drill masters and education has been seen as necessarily arduous and unpleasant.

The claims of the advocates of the formal discipline theory were not supported by any publically testable evidence. Quite to the contrary, later experimental findings indicated that neither drills and recitations nor studies in specific subjects in fact improved general mental capacities. Edward Thorndike states:

> . . . a change in one function alters any other only in so far as the two functions have as factors identical elements. The change in the second function is in amount that due to the change in the elements common to it and the first. The change is simply the necessary result upon the second function of the alteration of those of its factors which were elements of the first function, and so were altered by its training. To take a concrete example, improvement in addition will alter one's ability in multiplication because addition is absolutely identical with a part of multiplication and because certain other processes,—e.g., eye movements and the inhibition of all save arithmetical impulses,—are in part common to the two functions.[11]

Thorndike's experiments suggested that the amount of general improvement brought about by specific training was indeed very small and that there was no evidence to support the notion that some subjects had greater disciplinary value than others. This implies that the values of subjects must be determined by the special learning they lead to and that there is no valid empirical basis for asserting that some subjects

11. Edward L. Thorndike, *Educational Psychology*, Vol. II, *Psychology of Learning*, pp. 268–269.

contribute more to students' intellectual growth than others. According to Thorndike, transfer of learning occurs not because of strengthened faculties but because the original and new responses have "identical elements." If learning in a new situation occurs more easily because of what was learned earlier, it is only because the two situations or activities learned overlap. Learning, then, is always specific never general. If learning *appears* to be general, it is because new situations have much of the original situations in them. This is what Thorndike called the "principle of identical elements."

Today the "principle of identical elements" is no longer held by learning theorists, yet their accounts of the transfer of training are not too dissimilar, in spirit, to Thorndike's formulation. Behaviorists in general agree that transfer of training occurs when new stimuli have elements similar to the original stimuli or when there is an equivalence between the original and new stimuli and/or responses. Cognitively oriented psychologists expect a large measure of transfer when the learner perceives two learning situations as sharing certain common relationships (patterns and configurations) between their various elements. Pedagogically this means that

> if similarities between the content of one subject and another are explicitly taught, if the subjects contain identical elements (e.g., cognate words in several languages), or if general principles and their broad applicability are stressed in teaching, then the experience gained in study *is* more likely to be generalized to other appropriate subject areas. For example, stressing the derivation of English words in the study of Latin does increase English vocabulary; and making explicit the principles behind the skill of shooting at underwater targets measurably improves the ability to transfer the skill when water depth is changed.[12]

Whether we see transfer of learning in terms of similar elements in the stimuli or the learner's perception of common patterns of dynamic relationships between the original and

---

12. Bernard Berelson and Gary A. Steiner, *Human Behavior: An Inventory Of Scientific Findings*, p. 162.

new situations, we must reject the view that mental exercises strengthen faculties of the mind for automatic application to later tasks. A sound answer to the question "How does transfer of learning occur?" must be supported by empirical evidence, because it is an empirical, not a speculative, question about a matter of fact.

A word must be said here about the place of transfer of learning in teaching theories, because transfer of learning is not only a key concept in any theory of teaching but is also one of the fundamental aspects of formal education. Regardless of what theory of teaching we hold or what view of schooling we accept, most of us agree that the child's learning experiences in one situation—his school—should help him to learn new things and to cope with problems in different situations. Put simply, transfer of learning means that what one has learned in one situation does influence the learner's activities in a new and different situation. This means that if transfer of learning never occurs, children will have to be taught specifically what to do in every future situation they are likely to encounter. Effectiveness of this type of teaching (or learning) is indeed questionable, because we cannot determine beforehand just what specific situations any single child will encounter. Moreover, this kind of teaching is likely to lead to blind routines, which are too inflexible to be of much help in dealing with change and new situations. Clearly, the degree to which schooling affects the child's life depends to a large extent on the amount and quality of the transfer of learning.

Instruction, Drilling, and Testing

To the advocates of the formal discipline theory teaching did not stand for any single act, but consisted of three different procedures, viz., instruction, drilling, and testing. Instruction was thought of as the process of facilitating the learner's acquisition of knowledge, thereby strengthening his power of knowing. Hence, the chief objective of instruction was to impart knowledge, while drilling was to make clear what had already been learned. In other words, the material learned through instruction was made permanent by repetition and practice, i.e., drilling. Consequently, White recommended that in elementary schools drill should absorb a full three fifths of teaching time.[13] Testing, as a part of the teaching process, was to determine the results of instruction and drilling. "The test [then] is the eye of teaching; the guide and inspirer of teacher and pupil. It not only throws needed light upon the teacher's work, but also awakens interest, secures attention, and adds energy and persistence to the pupil's efforts."[14] These procedures, though separate, were not to be used independently of each other but to be applied in varying combinations, e.g., instruction and testing, drilling and testing. But it is important for the teacher to be clear about which of the three elements is to be his leading concern at any given time, because

> the three teaching processes give, when used separately, three distinct teaching exercises, to wit: instruction exercises, drill exercises, and test exercises. But in practice, as already noted, these teaching processes are more or less united, this being specially true of instruction and drilling, as in teaching the school arts. . . . Indeed, the union of instruction and drilling in teaching is so common that neither term is ever technically used to designate the exercise. On the contrary, such an exercise is called a Lesson. . . .
>   . . . The testing process is a necessary element in every instruction or drill exercise, but its place is subordinate and incidental. When testing is the chief purpose of an exercise, it is a test exercise, and is properly called Recitation.[15]

Though White claimed that instruction, drilling, and testing would give three distinct exercises, they all led to one objective, exercising the mental faculties. Unlike many of

13. White, *The Art of Teaching*, p. 53.
14. *Ibid.*
15. *Ibid.*, pp. 54, 55.

today's educators, the formal disciplinarians had nothing to say about teaching in relation to socialization or the process of enculturation, for teaching was conceived as strictly a mental process leading to a disciplined mind. In such a process the learner had very little or nothing to do with determining either the content or the method of teaching. In principle, no advocate of the formal discipline theory argued against such qualities as independence, initiative, self-expression, and creativity. But in practice, conformity and unquestioning obedience were valued as desirable personality traits in the learner. Effort, not understanding, was the key concept in the formal disciplinarian view of teaching and learning.

The Formal Discipline Theory Today

Today the formal discipline theory is practically dead, but the fact that there are still some educators who believe that studying certain subjects will discipline the mind and improve its general capacities indicates how profound the influence of this theory has been in American education. The formal discipline theory, or some version of it, can be traced back to the time of Plato, but it was in the nineteenth century that the theory enjoyed its widest acceptance. Around 1900 Edward L. Thorndike found some fifty books on education, picked at random, favored the disciplinarian view of the transfer of learning. The following are only four of several excerpts Thorndike cited in his book *Educational Psychology:*

> It is as a means of training the faculties or perception and generalization that the study of such a language as Latin in comparison with English is so valuable. [C. L. Morgan, *Psychology for Teachers*, p. 186]

> Arithmetic, if judiciously taught, forms in the pupil habits of mental attention, argumentative sequence, absolute accuracy, and satisfaction in truth as a result, that do not seem to spring

equally from the study of any other subject suitable to this elementary stage of instruction. [Joseph Payne, *Lectures on Education*, Vol. 1, p. 260]

Let us now examine in detail the advantages which a person who has taken the ordinary Bachelor's degree has derived from the study of classics. Aside from the discipline of the will, which comes from any hard work, we find the following: (1) His memory for facts has been strengthened by committing paradigms and learning a new vocabulary. (2) He has been obliged to formulate pretty distinctly a regular system of classified facts—the facts which form the material of the grammar—classified in due form under chapter, section, subsection and so on. This means that he has learned to remember things by their relations—a power which can hardly be acquired without practice informing or using such classified systems. (3) He has had his judgment broadened and strengthened by constant calls upon it to account for things which cannot be accounted for without its exercise. [E. H. Babbitt, *Methods of Teaching the Modern Languages*, p. 126]

The visual mental and manual powers are cultivated in combination, the eye being trained to see clearly and judge accurately, the mind to think, and the hand to record the appearance of the object seen, or the conceptions formed in the mind. Facility and skill in handicraft, and delicacy of manipulation, all depend largely upon the extent to which this hand and eye training has been fostered. The inventive and imaginative faculties are stimulated and exercised in design, and the graphic memory is strengthened by practice in memory drawing. The aesthetic judgment is brought into use, the power of discerning beauty, congruity, proportion, symmetry, is made stronger; and the love of the beautiful, inherent more or less in mankind, is greatly increased. [J. H. Morris, *Teaching and Organization* (edited by P. A. Barnett), pp. 63-64][16]

Although these passages were written in the late nineteenth and early twentieth centuries they all have a rather familiar ring to us. Almost everyone has known teachers who still regard teaching and learning as primarily a matter of exercis-

---

16. Thorndike, *Educational Psychology*, Vol. II, pp. 269–271.

ing the mental powers, and who think certain subjects have more disciplinary value and a greater transfer power than others. This author recalls a colleague, a professor of modern languages, who insisted on requiring a foreign language for everyone, because he believed that the study of a foreign language disciplined the student's mind to enable him to do well in other areas of academic work.

In recent years no serious-minded educator has explicitly advanced the formal discipline theory as was done by Emerson E. White and J. B. Wickersham in the late nineteenth century. Yet, the basic tenets of the theory are frequently found in the educational writings of such able thinkers as Robert M. Hutchins, Mortimer J. Adler, and others who are closely associated with the Council for Basic Education. For this reason our subsequent discussions will deal with views on education in general. Their implications for teaching should be clear. As might be expected, Hutchins, an avid critic of the so-called "life adjustment" programs in American public schools, argues that education is chiefly the development of man's intellectual powers. Therefore, we should concentrate on cultivating such mental capacities as understanding and judgment rather than on producing narrowly trained specialists, because "an intellect properly disciplined, an intellect properly habituated, is an intellect able to operate well in all fields. An education that consists of the cultivation of the intellectual virtues, therefore, is the most useful education."[17] With this view both Cardinal Newman, the nineteenth-century proponent of liberal education through universal knowledge, and Mortimer J. Adler concur. In the latter's words, "education is the process by which those powers (abilities, capacities) of men that are susceptible to habituation are perfected by good habits, through means artistically contrived, and employed by any man to help another or himself achieve the end in view (i.e., good habits)."[18] Adler

---

17. Robert M. Hutchins, *The Higher Learning in America*, p. 63.
18. Mortimer J. Adler, "In Defense of the Philosophy of Education," *Philosophies of Education*, Nelson B. Henry, ed., p. 209.

holds that the aims of education should be the same for everyone, because, among other reasons, all men have the same natural capacities, which are to be developed through good habituations, which also happen to be the same for all men. By good habituations Adler means those habits which conform to the natural tendencies of our mental faculties. For example, the tendency to think logically is a good habit in cultivating the power of logical thinking.[19] It is through exercises and activities that good habits are developed to actualize the powers. Adler's view of man is based on the premise that all men having the same specific nature have the same natural powers or capacities. And since all individual men have the same specific human nature, Adler concludes that they must have the same natural powers or capacities.[20]

From Adler's perspective, the content of what is to be learned should not be determined by the learner's personal interest but only by what is objectively necessary to cultivate mental powers. The nature of the natural capacities should indicate what is to be learned and how the powers are to be trained. It is not at all surprising that Hutchins, too, thought of the learner's self-expression as pedagogically undesirable, because it was allegedly the exact opposite of rigorous education, while he regarded the studies of grammar, mathematics, etc., as worthwhile, for they were believed to dis-

---

19. *Ibid.*, p. 244.
20. Adler stated his argument in the following syllogism:

Major [premise]: All individuals having the same specific nature have the same natural powers or capacities.
Minor [premise]: All individual men have the same specific human nature.
Conclusion: All individual men have the same natural powers or capacities. *Ibid.*, p. 242.

In examining Adler's argument we find that the conclusion is logically valid, because it follows necessarily from the given premises. But the conclusion seems to be either tautologous or definitional and therefore it does not assert any matter of fact about man. In other words, the premise "All individuals having the same specific nature" is either defined as being the same as "having the same natural power or capacities," or the concept "same specific nature" already contains the notion of "same natural powers or capacities." Therefore, the premises and the conclusion are true in exactly the same sense in which the statement "Black is black" is true.

cipline the mind and develop its logical faculty.[21] In 1957 similar conclusions were reported by George H. Hyram and Robert B. Skelton in the results of their studies on the transfer value of studying logic and foreign language. In conducting his study, "An Experiment in Developing Critical Thinking in Children," Hyram defined critical thinking as essentially logical thinking, i.e., thinking according to the rules of formal deductive logic. As a means of developing the power of logical thinking, Hyram suggested that "upper grade pupils can be taught to think critically [logically] through the use of instructional procedures which emphasized the principles of logic as learning content."[22] If training in critical thinking were to become an objective of education to be realized through direct teaching efforts, teachers themselves must become proficient in the knowledge and use of logic.[23] In a separate study, Robert B. Skelton claimed that "the study of foreign language does improve one's command of his own language, thereby enhancing one's control of subject matter in fields in which language is the vehicle of instruction."[24] This conclusion was based on the findings of his study "High-School Foreign Language Study and Freshman Performance," which showed a significantly high correlation between foreign language students and superior academic achievements. In other words, foreign language students as a group performed better academically than non-foreign language students, and Skelton concluded that the study of a foreign language causally contributed to the superior academic performance on the part of foreign language students. There are many critical comments we can make about these studies, but let us limit our analysis to two points which are relevant to our discussion here. As was stated earlier, Hyram claimed that the

21. Hutchins, *Learning in America*, pp. 82–84.
22. George H. Hyram, "An Experiment in Developing Critical Thinking in Children," *Journal of Experimental Education*, December, 1957, p. 130.
23. *Ibid.*, p. 131.
24. Robert G. Skelton, "High-School Foreign Language Study and Freshman Performance," *School and Society*, June 8, 1957, p. 205.

study of logic improves the learner's critical thinking ability. But we should note that critical thinking was defined as logical thinking, i.e., thinking according to the rules of logic. According to Hyram's definition, "logical thinking does depend upon a knowledge of the principles of logic."[25] The transfer of learning from studying logic to critical thinking occurs not because logic strengthens the power of reasoning but because critical thinking and logical thinking mean the same. The statement that "logical thinking does depend upon a knowledge of the principles of logic" does not require an experimental study to determine its validity, for the very definition of logical thinking makes the statement true. As to Skelton's study, one may indeed find a high correlation between foreign language study and high academic achievement, but this does not necessarily imply that the former is causally related to the latter. Hence, to say that the study of a foreign language will improve one's academic performance is simply fallacious, for correlational data tell us only about the "degree of going togetherness." The purpose for citing these two studies is to show that even today there are educators who hold views that are extremely similar to the formal discipline theory of teaching.

As we have already seen, the exponents of the formal discipline theory did not regard imparting useful knowledge as their primary concern in teaching. To them, practical skills and knowledge had very limited value, because only properly trained faculties could enable a person to function in all fields. The training of mental powers was their most important educational objective and the cultivation of intellectual powers was believed to be accomplished best by exercising the appropriate faculties. This meant that the teacher's primary responsibility was not to cater to the learner's own desires but to find and introduce those materials and activities which were best suited to disciplining the various faculties. Though this view of teaching was consistent with a number of

25. Hyram, "Developing Critical Thinking in Children," p. 130.

different curricular arrangements, by the nineteenth century the classical curriculum was widely accepted as the best and the most effective means of training the mind. The classical curriculum, consisting of the "great" works in philosophy, literature, and science, was believed to be the most important source from which one could gain eternal wisdom and unchanging knowledge about Truth, Goodness, and Beauty as discovered and recorded by the greatest minds of the West. The classical curriculum was consonant with not only the psychological basis of the formal discipline theory (faculty psychology) but also with its philosophical premise that man possessed a mind, a nonphysical entity, which made him distinct from other forms of animals.

FACULTY PSYCHOLOGY

If education is seen essentially as a process by which the mental powers (faculties) are strengthened and developed, what psychologists have to say about the nature of the mind and its functions is directly relevant to the discussion of the teaching-learning process. Although the formal discipline theory of teaching does not logically and necessarily follow from any single school of psychology, the advocates of the theory consistently referred to faculty psychology as the basis of their claims. Faculty psychology, which prevailed on the Continent from the middle of the eighteenth century through most of the nineteenth century, was conceived by its proponents as a science of the mind or soul and of its connection with the human body. Faculty psychologists held that their discipline was based on "exact observation, precise definition, fixed terminology, classified arrangement, and rational explanation."[26] Of course, what they meant by "exact observation, precise definition," etc., does not conform to the criteria of evidence and verification as found in the empirical

26. Porter, *The Human Intellect*, p. 2.

sciences today. In terms of today's standards the so-called "rational explanations" are too metaphysical, too speculative, to be regarded as scientific explanations. Nevertheless, faculty psychology was an attempt to incorporate certain empirical elements into psychology, thereby partially divorcing it from philosophy. For this reason faculty psychology was a curious mixture of speculative philosophy and observational data about man's mental activities.

The basic tenet of faculty psychology is the belief that man's mind as an entity possesses a number of faculties, powers, or what Christian von Wolff called the "potencies of action," which are believed to be responsible for carrying out such mental functions as remembering, reasoning, willing, and understanding. As Thomas Reid put it:

> We are conscious that we think, and that we have a variety of thoughts of different kinds; such as seeing, hearing, remembering, deliberating, resolving, loving, hating, and many other kinds of thought, all which we are taught by nature to attribute to an internal principle; and this principle of thought we call the mind or soul of a man."[27]

As we know certain properties of our body through its operations, so we can know about the mind from its functions. In other words, from the fact that man can perform these mental activities we can infer the existence of corresponding faculties or powers, because

> every operation supposes a power in the being that operates; for to suppose any thing to operate which has no power to operate is manifestly absurd. But, on the other hand, there is no absurdity in supposing a being to have power to operate when it does not operate. Thus, I may have power to walk when I sit, or to speak when I am silent. Every operation, therefore, implies power; but the power does not imply operation.[28]

The term *faculties* does not simply describe human activities,

27. Walker, *Reid's Essays*, p. 5.
28. *Ibid.*, p. 6.

but stands for powers, nonphysical entities, which are inherent in all men. The central concern of faculty psychology is to study the nature and function of these powers.

Historically, there was a wide range in the number of faculties attributed to the mind. For example, Wolff held that the mind consisted of two major powers: (1) understanding or knowing and (2) willing or desiring. In elaborating Wolff's classification Reid stated:

> Under the will we comprehend our active powers, and all that lead to action, or influence the mind to act, such as appetites, passions, affections. The understanding comprehends our contemplative powers; by which we perceive objects; by which we conceive or remember them; by which we analyze or compound them; and by which we judge and reason concerning them.[29]

In other words, the power of knowing was made up of the faculties of perception, memory, understanding, and reason, while the power of willing included such faculties as feeling, desiring, loving, and hating. Jouffroy, a contemporary of Reid, named the following six faculties: (1) the personal faculty or liberty or will, (2) the primitive inclinations, (3) the locomotive faculty, (4) the expressive faculty, (5) sensibility, and (6) the intellectual faculty.[30] But Noah Porter suggested that the leading faculties of the intellect were three: "the presentative, or observing faculty; the representative, or creative faculty; the thinking, or the generalizing faculty. More briefly, the faculty of experience, the faculty of representation, and the faculty of intelligence."[31] But whatever the classification one held, it was not to be assumed that the faculties could be known completely, for man's knowledge of the division of the mind was recognized as imperfect. Therefore, Reid insisted that we "leave room for such additions or alterations as a more perfect view of the subject may afterwards suggest."[32]

29. *Ibid.*, p. 28.
30. *Ibid.*, p. 30.
31. Porter, *The Human Intellect*, p. 77.
32. Walker, *Reid's Essays*, p. 31.

Faculties of the mind, though separate, did not function independently of each other. And while different faculties often functioned jointly, man's physical state could still be said to be predominately in the state of feeling or thinking or willing. Similarly, though the faculties were believed to develop sequentially, developmental stages could overlap, so the child might perceive and remember at the same time. If each faculty had to be completely matured before another faculty could develop, we would have to say that the child perceives with the senses for a long time before he begins to remember, and that he remembers and imagines for another long period before he can generalize and reason. This would indeed be an absurd view of mental development, because, if it were true, a young child could not reason, since the power of reasoning is said to develop toward the latter part of the child's mental growth. The fact that faculties are not entirely independent of one another suggests that they should not be trained separately, because "the soul with a structure abnormal, cannot attain a healthy and shapely growth. Any striking predominance of the intellectual over the emotional powers, or any defect in energy of will, either prevents even progress, or induces premature feebleness or a dwarfish stature."[33] For faculty psychologists, the primary objective of education was to train the powers of the mind to work in harmony, because education was more than the transmission of knowledge. It was also thought to be the process of developing the sensibilities to guide man's action and form his character.

Learning

Because it was bound up with speculative and metaphysical interest in the nature of man's soul, faculty psychology, unlike contemporary psychology, did not consider learning as a major concern. How faculty psychologists saw learning, then, has to be examined in terms of their views on the training of

---

33. Porter, *The Human Intellect*, p. 33.

the mental powers and the conditions which were believed to be conducive for such development. Like the formal disciplinarians, Thomas Reid suggested that the most effective means of cultivating the faculties was through appropriate exercises. For example, exercising of the reasoning power not only strengthens the faculty but also "furnishes the mind with a store of materials. Every train of reasoning which is familiar becomes a beaten track in the way to many others. It removes many obstacles which lay in our way, and smooths many roads which we may have occasion to travel in future disquisition."[34] However, the exercise was not to be accomplished at random but by following certain rules according to which the faculty operates. For instance, Noah Porter listed (1) energy, contrast, and resemblance; (2) motion; (3) repetition; and (4) familiarity[35] as rules related to the growth of the powers of perception and memory. By energy, contrast, and resemblance, Porter meant that subjects are more likely to be perceived when they are either very similar or very dissimilar and contrasts between the perceived objects are made more clear and definite by their (objects') motion. Repetition was thought of as an efficient and often an indispensable condition for the completion of an act of perception. Even such simple sense data as sound, color, and taste were said to be more perfectly mastered by being apprehended in successive acts of attention. Further, familiar objects would be more readily perceived, while novel and unfamiliar objects were more slowly and often painfully grasped. The rules of memory then can be stated in the following form:

> To remember anything, you must attend to it; and in order to attend, you must either find or create an interest in the objects to be attended to. This interest must, if possible, be felt in the objects themselves, as directly related to your own wishes, feelings, and purposes, and not to some remote end on account of which you desire to make acquisition.[36]

34. Walker, *Reid's Essays*, p. 425.
35. Porter, *The Human Intellect*, pp. 200–207.
36. *Ibid.*, p. 321.

In other words, when studying a new subject we must feel that the knowledge to be gained from the study is for ourselves and that we may eagerly satisfy our mind with freshness and zest. Porter tried to formulate a set of laws of association by which we can learn to perceive and to remember. These laws were explained in terms of (1) the connectedness of objects, (2) contiguity of perception and (3) the resemblance between current and previous perceptual experiences. This formulation is reminiscent of the claim of David Hume, the eighteenth-century British empiricist philosopher, that contiguity, conjunction, resemblance of events, and the notion of cause and effect are the basis of association of ideas. As for the faculty of reasoning, the laws of thought were believed to be identical with the criteria of correct thinking, namely, the rules of logic.[37] Learning, as viewed by faculty psychologists, was a process of influencing man's mental activities by exercising the various faculties of the mind according to certain fixed laws of association and correct thinking. As some readers may have already noted, these laws of learning are almost identical with the rules of teaching as suggested by the advocates of the formal discipline theory. It would appear that the instructional principles of the formal discipline theory are elaborations of faculty psychology in the specific context of school learning.

Faculty Psychology Today

In spite of its disrepute, faculty psychology is not completely without its defenders today. The notion of the mind as an entity with various powers and the concept of teaching and learning as involving vigorous exercise of these powers are quite congenial to our common sense beliefs about man's

---

37. We must be careful to distinguish the "laws of correct thinking" from the "laws of thinking." The laws of correct thinking are logical rules which "tell us" how we ought to think. But the laws of thinking are psychological "laws" which describe how people in fact think.

mind and its education. But not all support for faculty psychology comes from the man in the street, for there are a number of able thinkers who seriously hold that faculty psychology is neither outdated nor unscientific. Raymond J. Anable, author of *Philosophical Psychology,* insists that faculty psychology "is not outmoded unless modern psychology has found a better method. It is not unscientific if it is based on facts, and the conclusions it draws are logically warranted by these facts."[38] Of course, what is meant by a "better method" and "facts" depends upon one's view of knowledge and, fundamentally, upon one's world view. What is factual and scientific to a Thomist may indeed be only poetic and fictitious to an empiricist. In any event, Anable is convinced that man is endowed with various mental faculties or powers because he carries on different mental operations. In other words, "any activity presupposes that the being exercising that activity has the power or faculty for that specific activity, and radically different kinds of activity presuppose different powers or faculties."[39] But it is "I" or the mind rather than faculties which actually performs varied conscious acts. "These acts are [then] the key to the powers 'I' must have, and since these powers or faculties are *mine* (are man's), their perfection is indicative of the perfection and grade and manner of being of the one whose faculties they are."[40]

Thus, to Anable, the fact that man carries on conscious mental functions logically and necessarily implies the existence of (1) faculties as entities, and (2) "I," yet another entity, because of which man performs his conscious activities. As fundamental as these assumptions are to faculty psychology, they are the sort of premises which empirically oriented psychologists and philosophers find impossible to defend. Yet Mortimer J. Adler argues that the doctrine of faculties has been misunderstood and unjustly attacked in

38. Raymond J. Anable, *Philosophical Psychology,* p. 97.
39. *Ibid.,* p. 100.
40. *Ibid.,* pp. 100–101.

recent years. From Adler's point of view an accurate understanding of the concept of faculty must take into account:

(1) that the faculties are powers of operation, i.e., abilities and capacities. . . .
(2) that the faculties or powers are neither parts of the essence of soul nor separate from the soul as independent agents, but rather distinctions within the total power of the soul. . . .
(3) that the distinction of the faculties from each other and from the soul, which is their principle, is real rather than formal. . . . Faculties, being accidents, cannot exist independently of their subject, man, but they are really distinct from their principle, the soul, as is clear from their independent variability. . . .
(4) that the faculties are not that which act but that in virtue of which man acts. . . .[41]

Therefore, faculties are not mere fictions, nor do they stand for dispositions or descriptions of human behavior.

By now it should be clear that the modern account of faculties as given by Anable and Adler is essentially the same as the views held by earlier faculty psychologists. Central to faculty psychology, historical or contemporary, is the belief that the human mind with its powers exists as a nonphysical entity distinct from the body. In other words, the substantive view of the mind is the philosophical cornerstone which supports faculty psychology. Consequently, a critical examination of the substantive view of the mind is essential to any serious analysis of faculty psychology.

THE SUBSTANTIVE VIEW OF MIND

The Mind As a Substance

The substantive view of the mind is founded on the belief that the mind is a nonphysical substance which is distinct from the body, a physical substance. The term *substance* does not stand for material existence but it refers to that which exists in and by itself. This means that mind and body as two

---

41. Mortimer J. Adler, *What Man Has Made of Man*, pp. 79–80.

different substances exist separately. Their existence is neither contingent upon nor reducible to each other. As Descartes pointed out, man is made up of two "things," a thinking "thing" and a physical "thing." The mind as a thinking "thing" is called *unextended*[42] because it has no physical properties, while the body is said to be *extended* because it has sensible qualities. It is not difficult to see oneself as a physical thing, a body, but what is a thinking thing? "It is a thing which doubts, understands, conceives, affirms, denies, wills, refuses, which also imagines and feels."[43] Descartes reasoned that since man carries on these mental activities there must be some "thing" which is responsible for them. And the thing which enables man to perform his conscious acts is called the mind, an *unextended substance*.[44] It is no wonder that the substantive view of the mind has been so influential in the West, because we naturally think of our mind as a non-physical thing which unifies and organizes our daily experiences. We also speak of the mind as the agent that experiences, thinks, and feels. Further, most of us believe that the mind is permanent and indestructible even by physical death. Indeed we could call the substantive view "common-sense substantialism" or "common-sense dualism." Yet, the idea of unextended substance is still puzzling. We can readily understand the nature of extended substance, because it has qualities that can be known through sense experience, but an entity which has no physical properties is completely alien to our experience.

Objections to the Substantive View

To an empiricist like David Hume, our ideas about matters of fact come from (1) direct sense data or (2) inferences based on sense data. This means that there can be no purely speculative and/or a priori ideas about matters of fact. From

42. The expression "unextended substance" is used interchangeably with "substance," "soul substance," "mind substance," or "metaphysical substance."
43. Ralph M. Eaton, ed., *Descartes Selections*, p. 100.
44. *Ibid.*, p. 24.

such a point of view the mind as a nonphysical entity could not exist, because the expression "unextended substance" is meaningless. That is, the term has no informative meaning, because it is not based on either our sense data or inferences from them. Consequently, *unextended substance* does not stand for any actual entity. Moreover, as Hume argues, whenever we are conscious of ourselves we are always aware of some particular sensations of heat, cold, pain, love, hatred, pleasure, etc. But we never perceive what we call our "self" or the mind. Hence, Hume concluded that the mind is nothing more than a collection of sensations rather than a nonphysical entity. We will be discussing the Humean view of the mind in greater detail in the following chapter, but whether we agree or disagree with Hume, his position raises perhaps the most fundamental question regarding the basis for the substantive view. If we can show that *unextended substance* is indeed meaningless, the substantive view has no foundation.

To Gilbert Ryle, a twentieth-century analytic philosopher, the term *mind* does not stand for any "thing"; it is just an expression for talking about certain types of human behavior. The notion that man has both a body and a mind "is one big mistake and a mistake of a special kind. It is, namely, a category-mistake. It represents the facts of mental life as if they belong to one logical type or category (or range of types or categories), when they actually belong to another."[45] In other words, the proponents of the substantive view mistook the term *mind* to be in the same category as the term *body.* And since terms like *body, orange, arms,* and *chairs* have concrete objects as their referents, they assumed that the term *mind* also must have an object as its referent. To be sure, this referent object was unlike any other physical object. But for Ryle, the term *mind* belongs to a logical category in which terms such as *team spirit, courage, corporation,* etc., belong. These descriptive terms are without objects as their referents.

45. Gilbert Ryle, *The Concept of Mind*, p. 16.

The following illustration of Ryle may further clarify what he means by the phrase *category-mistake:*

> A foreigner visiting Oxford or Cambridge for the first time is shown a number of colleges, libraries, playing fields, museums, scientific departments and administrative offices. He then asks 'But where is the University? I have seen where the members of the Colleges live, where the Registrar works, where the scientists experiment and the rest. But I have not yet seen the University in which reside and work the members of your University.' It has then to be explained to him that the University is not another collateral institution, some ulterior counterpart to the colleges, laboratories and offices which he has seen. The University is just the way in which all that he has already seen is organized. When they are seen and when their co-ordination is understood, the University has been seen. His mistake lay in his innocent assumption that it was correct to speak of Christ Church, the Bodeleian Library, the Ashmolean Museum *and* the University, to speak, that is, as if 'the University stood for an extra member of the class of which these other units are members.' He was mistakenly allocating the University to the same category as that to which the other institutions belong.[46]

As the term *university* describes the way in which libraries, administrative offices, laboratories, etc., are organized, so does the term *mind* describe man's intelligent behavior. The category mistake, according to Ryle, seems to have been made because the advocates of the substantive view erroneously reasoned that since our physical functions are explained in terms of certain physical entities and their operations (eyes see, legs walk, etc.), it was assumed that mental activities like thinking, reasoning, and remembering must also be functions of another entity with properties that are quite different from our body. Consequently,

> the differences between the physical and the mental were thus represented as differences inside the common framework of the

46. *Ibid.*, p. 16.

categories of "thing," "stuff," "attitude," "process," "change," "cause," and "effect." Minds are things, but different sorts of things from bodies. . . . That this assumption was at the heart of the [substantive] doctrine [of the mind] is known by the fact that there was from the beginning felt to be a major theoretical difficulty in explaining how minds can influence and be influenced by bodies.[47]

What Ryle is suggesting is that if we correct the category-mistake and place the term *mind* in its proper category as describing certain types of human behavior, we will no longer have the problem of explaining how minds and bodies as unextended and extended substances can causally influence each other. According to Ryle, "the hallowed contrast between Mind and Matter will be dissipated, but dissipated not by either of the equally hallowed absorptions of Mind by Matter or of Matter by Mind, but in quite a different way. For the seeming contrast of the two will be shown to be as illegitimate as would be the contrast of 'she came home in a flood of tears' and 'she came home in a sedan-chair.'"[48] Ryle, of course, is not attempting to show that we can make no distinction between the mental and the physical. But he does want to point out that the mind is not a mysterious entity which animates the body to think, to reason, to recall, etc. There is no "ghost in the machine." We can indeed say "I have a mind," but only as a figure of speech having a logically different meaning than the statement "I have a body."

Ryle's persuasive argument against the substantive view of the mind is based fundamentally on the empiricist criteria of knowledge. Therefore, all ideas about matters of fact must come those human experiences which are intersubjectively testable. But to the advocates of the substantive doctrine such criteria of knowledge are too limited and Ryle's arguments would have little force. Proponents of the substantive view may agree with Ryle that people often do make

47. *Ibid.*, p. 19.
48. *Ibid.*, p. 22.

category-mistakes and that certain words are often mistakenly reified (hypostatized). But the fact that people make category-mistakes does not imply that the notion of substantial mind is an instance of such a mistake. Hence, the substantialists argue that their view has not been conclusively refuted.

The Mind-Body Relationship

Two-sided Interactionism From this puzzling problem regarding the nature of mind we now turn to a discussion of the relationship between mind and body. Though the substantialists see mind and body as two distinct and independent entities, neither of which is reducible to the other, they believed these different substances to causally act upon each other. This view of the mind-body relation is called two-sided or dualistic interactionism. Like the substantive view, two-sided interactionism appears to be beyond any dispute, for it seems to agree so closely with our everyday experiences. For example, we can decide to run and our legs move. We can also recall those instances in which our thought processes have been seriously affected by poor physical conditions or drugs. Our lives are so full of these commonplace experiences that many people find it difficult to see anything other than two-sided interactionism as giving us an adequate account of the mind-body relationship. Yet, what is puzzling about this dualistic view is that if mind and body are so radically different from each other, how can there be any interaction between them? They share no common properties which are relevant to such causal relationship. We can understand how a rock can be crushed with a hammer or how our hands can move an object, because all of them have physical properties. But how can a thought or a thought-like thing move a physical object? According to Descartes, the mind-body connection is made by very minute and rapidly moving particles of the blood in a very small gland suspended in the middle of the brain. But Descartes' account showed only how one extended substance, the particles, affected another extended substance, the gland. It did not address itself to, and hence could not explain, the question of how interaction could occur between an extended substance (the body) and an unextended one (the mind).

Interactionism: Objections and Replies

Inconceivability One of the principal objections raised against dualistic interactionism is that any cause-effect relation between two entities which are so fundamentally different is outside of human experience and therefore we are ignorant of how supposed interaction takes place. We know that physical entities and events are causally influenced by other physical objects and processes that are capable of exerting physical force. If physical force is a product of mass and acceleration, how can a nonphysical "thing" which has no mass causally influence a physical object? We cannot understand how an entity such as the mind which has neither mass nor capability of acceleration can affect our physical body, for these two substances do not share any common characteristics relevant to such a causal relation. Hence, to noninteractionists any reciprocal cause-effect relation between mind and body is inconceivable and unintelligible.

To the proponents of dualistic interactionism, neither human ignorance nor "inconceivability" presents a serious threat to their position, because, as they point out, human history is full of instances in which what was once thought impossible became fact. They argue further that there are many natural phenomena that are as mysterious as the mind-body interaction. For example, we do not understand the actual *how* of the gravitational attraction, that is, how does "action at a distance" occur between two bodies that are millions of miles away? Accordingly, as contemporary dualists C. D. Broad and A. C. Ewing suggest, our inability to conceive of interaction between extended and unextended substances is not a sufficient condition for rejecting either the substantive view or two-sided interactionism, for "we cannot know a priori what degree of difference is incompatible with causal connection. The fact that we cannot see why the connection holds is no good ground for supposing that it does not hold. Even in the case of two ordinary physical things which are generally admitted to interact we cannot see why they should do so."[49] This reply is reinforced by C. J. Ducasse's retort that the causal principle does not require that causes and effects must both belong to the same ontological category as long as they are events.[50] In other words, there is nothing in the causal principle that requires causes and effects to be either all mental or all physical. The mind-body interaction is not contrary to the cause-effect principle. Moreover, as C. D. Broad adds,

> we must . . . admit the possibility that minds and mental events have properties and relations which do not reveal themselves to introspection, and that bodies and bodily events may have properties and relations which do not reveal themselves to perception or to physical and chemical experiment. In virtue of these properties and relations the two together may well form a single substantial whole of the kind which is alleged to be needed for causal interaction. Thus, if we accept the premise of the argument, we have no right to assert that mind and body cannot interact; but only the much more modest proposition that introspection and perception do not suffice to assure us that mind and body are so interrelated that they can interact.[51]

As contemporary interactionists insist, we should not reject interactionism just because we do not understand how such diverse entities as minds and bodies can influence each other.

49. A. C. Ewing, *Non-Linguistic Philosophy*, p. 167. C. D. Broad makes a similar comment in his book, *The Mind and Its Place in Nature*, pp. 97–98.
50. Curt Ducasse, "In Defense of Dualism," *Dimensions of Mind*, Sidney Hook, ed., p. 88.
51. Broad, *The Mind in Nature*, p. 100.

But does this imply that the interactionist position is valid? The answer is no. If we do not understand how mind and body can affect each other, this means precisely that we *do not* understand such a causal relation. Neither human ignorance nor "inconceivability" should be sufficient grounds for accepting or rejecting a point of view. This means that the most we can say about the mind-body interaction is that such a relation may or may not exist, and these replies give no positive support for the interactionist position. But how does Ducasse's comment on the causal principle affect the interactionist argument?

Ducasse was correct in reminding us that the causal principle does not require that causes and effects be part of a single or the same order of existence. To Ducasse this meant that mind and body as representing two independent orders of existence could influence each other. But does his argument establish the fact of mind-body interaction? Let us consider the causal principle and see how it affects interactionism. The so-called causal principle, viz., the belief that every event has a cause(s) and effect(s), is not an empirical generalization about how nature operates. We postulate the principle because by doing so the world we perceive "becomes" intelligible and orderly. Because it is a basic assumption, neither empirical nor logical proof of it is possible; that is, any scientific attempt to demonstrate the validity of the causal law must presuppose it, because the scientific method of investigation is founded on the premise that all events are caused. On the other hand, the fact that events occur does not by itself indicate to us that they are necessarily caused. Without postulating this principle, however, the universe will appear as a collection of disconnected and fragmented events without any meaning. The causal principle as an assumption then suggests to us that *we ought to* see events as having causes and effects. But it does not inform us about which specific events can, or do in fact, causally influence which other events, for such knowledge about events must come from empirical investigation of actual situations. Therefore, unless Ducasse can show by observation and experiment that minds and bodies actually interact with each other, his comments regarding the causal principle do not establish the fact of mind-body interaction. At best, Ducasse's argument indicates that if minds and bodies in fact influence each other causally, such relation is not contrary to the causal principle. Even if we agree with Broad that minds and bodies *may* have certain unobserved properties which make their interaction possible, we are still far away from establishing the truth of two-sided interactionism in any definitive sense, because Broad's statements are only about what *may* or *may not* be the case.

The Conservation of Energy Principle From the empiricist point of view two-sided interaction between minds and bodies is untenable because such a causal relationship violates the principle of conservation of energy. In brief, this principle states that the amount of energy in any closed physical system is constant and, therefore, the total amount of energy can be neither increased nor decreased. Now if a mental event did cause a physical event, the mental energy involved in the bodily occurence is expended and, hence, energy is lost. Similarly, a physical event causing a mental event will alter the amount of energy in the physical system. For example, if I decide to move my head and then carry out this intention into action, what began as a mental event terminates in a physical event, and it would seem that some amount of energy has been added to the physical system. If, conversely, some physical event such as a loud noise results in a perception of sound within my consciousness, energy from the material world would seem to have been "lost." In any case, the total amount of energy is changed and the principle of conservation of energy is violated. And since the principle is one of the most fundamental and inclusive rules of science, we have sufficient grounds for saying that causal connections between minds and bodies are not possible and that two-sided interactionism must be false.

To this scientific objection Ducasse responds by pointing out that:

> (A) . . . the conservation which that principle asserts is not something known to be true without exception, but is . . . only a defining postulate of the notion of a *wholly closed* physical world, so that the question whether psycho-physical or physico-psychical causation ever occurs is (but in different words) the question whether the physical world *is* wholly closed. And that question is not answered by dignifying as a "principle" the assumption that the physical world is wholly closed.
>
> (B) Anyway, . . . it might be the case that whenever a given amount of energy vanishes from, or emerges in, the physical world at one place, then an equal amount of energy respectively emerges in, or vanishes from, that world at another place.
>
> (C) And thirdly, if "energy" is meant to designate something experimentally measurable, then "energy" is defined in terms of causality, *not* "causality" in terms of transfer of energy. That is, it is not known that *all* causation, or, in particular, causation as between psychical and physical events, involves transfer of energy.[52]

Like the causal "law," the principle of conservation of energy is not a statement of an empirical fact but it is a postulate, an assumption, we make about a "wholly closed physical world." And this sort of assumption does not suggest that causal relationship between the physical and the mental does or does not occur. Moreover, the amount of energy in the system may remain constant because a loss of energy in one part of the world is followed by emergence of an equal amount of energy at another place in the world. Further, there is nothing in the concept of causation to indicate that causal relationship between minds and bodies must involve transfer of energy. To the substantialist this empirical argument would have little force, for the mind as an unextended substance is not likely to be subject to the conservation of energy principle, because an unextended substance does not have any of the physical

---

52. Ducasse, *In Defense of Dualism*, p. 89.

properties material objects have. It is possible, then, that the mind-body interaction can be explained in terms of laws and principles that are fundamentally different from the laws of the physical world.

Ducasse rightly claims that the conservation of energy principle is not a statement of fact about the universe, but even as an assumption about the physical world it does have explanatory and predictive power and we have not yet found any good reason to reject the principle. Therefore, if we can show that interactionism actually violates the principle, we may reject the interactionist position. Now the crucial question is whether or not the mind-body interaction in fact alters the total amount of energy in the system. Again, Ducasse correctly points out that there is nothing in the causal principle that indicates that the causal relation between mind and body necessarily involves any loss or gain of energy. But since our question is about causal connections between physical and nonphysical entities, empirical investigation will be of little help to us. In short, we do not have sufficient grounds for insisting that interactionism does in fact violate the conservation of energy principle, nor do we have any good reason to deny that the principle was not violated. Ducasse has shown that his critics have failed to refute dualistic interactionism conclusively. But this in no way demonstrates that Ducasse's own position is valid.

Though Broad, Ducasse, and Ewing are adamant in arguing that their critics have failed to refute two-sided interactionism conclusively, they have not given us positive proofs for the mind-body interaction. Furthermore, even if interactionists can demonstrate that the objections raised by their adversaries are completely false, this alone does not make dualistic interactionism valid. For example, our inability to disprove conclusively the claim that three angels could stand on the head of a pin does not imply that three angels can in fact stand on the head of a pin or that angels exist at all. Similarly, noninteractionists' failure to disprove dualistic interactionism does not add one iota of validity to the notion that mind and body can causally influence each other. Even Ducasse's own concept of the mind "as consisting, like material substance, of sets of systematically interrelated dispositions, i.e., of capacities, abilities, powers, and susceptibilities,"[53] will not save mind-body dualism. If these dispositions are seen as belonging to a single substance we no longer have dualism. But if they are thought of as separate entities we are led to a curious form of pluralism, because dispositions are usually regarded as states or tendencies but not as "things." In any event, the cause of dualistic interactionism is not helped by Ducasse's view.

Parallelism   One way of escaping the objections we have discussed thus far is to deny that mind and body influence each other. Accordingly, some philosophers contended that there was no real causal relationship between minds and bodies. Mind and body functioned separately and independently from each other, and, therefore, they represented two causally unrelated series of events existing in perfect parallel. This then is the basic tenet of *parallelism* in a nutshell. However, not all parallelists[54] agreed on the nature of this parallel relationship. *Occasionalists* held that the occurence of a mental (or physical) event becomes an occasion for God to intervene and produce an appropriate (mental or physical) event. But there were others who held that mental and physical events occur according to a certain pre-established sequence, so changes in one realm were paralleled by changes in the other without involving any cause-effect relation between them. This *pre-established harmony* or synchronization between the mental and the physical was presumbly the work of a divine being.

As might be expected, parallelism has often been accused of being absurd, because it is so contrary to our day-by-day experiences. Hence, we may object by insisting that the denial

---

53. *Ibid.*, p. 90.
54. Historically, Malebranche and Leibnitz represented occasionalism and the doctrine of pre-established harmony, respectively.

of man's commonplace experiences is too much of a price to pay to "save" dualism. We may further argue that if the parallelist position, i.e., the doctrine of pre-established harmony, is followed to its logical conclusion, we will be led to some form of panpsychism, a monistic view which asserts that everything is mental in nature; for, if mental events so perfectly parallel physical events, the same relationship must exist between physical and mental events. We are then forced to conclude that there is mind in everything. Unfortunately, panpsychism of any sort will not help the parallelist cause, because it is a monistic, not a dualistic, view.

What is common about occasionalism and the doctrine of pre-established harmony is the fact that in both instances God is used to explain the mind-body relation. That is, the parallel relationship between mind and body is attributed to the work of an unseen being, God. Such an entity is called a *theoretical entity* or a *construct,* because it is an unobserved and unobservable entity postulated as a part of a theoretical explanation of some observed phenomena. As such, a theoretical construct may be used legitimately when its postulation is likely to increase (1) our knowledge of the phenomena under investigation and/or (2) the predictive power of the explanation. On the other hand, if the postulated entity, God in this case, contributes neither to the growth of our knowledge nor to the increase in the predictive power of our knowledge, the construct should not be introduced. Applying these criteria to both parallelist views, we find that postulation of God would not increase our knowledge about the causal relationship between minds and bodies, nor would it give us an added power for predicting future mental and/or physical events. Therefore, we may reject occasionalism and the doctrine of pre-established harmony. These parallelist views, it seems to me, are not explanations of the mind-body regularities as much as desperate attempts to "save" dualism by eliminating certain objectionable elements in the theory of two-sided interactionism.

CONCLUDING COMMENTS

THE FORMAL DISCIPLINE THEORY

Contrary to our current interest in making education meaningful by relating school learning to the needs, aptitudes, and aspirations of the learner, the proponents of the formal discipline theory had little or no concern in selecting the curricular materials and activities in cooperation with the learner. Subject matter was seen primarily as material with which to train the child's mental powers. Hence, everyone underwent the same program. Since the training of the mental capacities required strict discipline, drills, and recitations, conformity and unquestioning obedience on the part of the learner were virtues of the day. This meant that qualities such as self-expression, creativity, self-reliance, and initiative were neglected. Although the curricular content gained increasing importance, simply because the mental exercises necessarily involved working with subject matter, the formal disciplinarians saw little need for an expanded curriculum. The notion that teaching is an intellectual as well as a socio-cultural and moral process was alien to the proponents of the formal discipline theory.

The advocates of the discipline theory were concerned with avoiding narrow and stilted education, but the balanced education of the child was to be achieved through harmonious development of the faculties by properly distributed mental exercises. The fact that meaningful education must involve the learner's experience of integrating his intellectual activities with the socio-cultural and moral dimensions of the school and society simply did not occur to the disciplinarians. It is this predominantly intellectual approach to teaching that eventually led to the traditional educational practices based on barren formalism in which effort (hard work) and rigidly prescribed exercises for mental gymnastics acquired prime importance. But man does not live by his intellect alone. His personality, his intelligence, his values and attitudes are acquired through and cultivated by very complex psychological and cultural processes. It is through education as a deliberate enculturative and acculturative process that each man evolves into a social being and each society perpetuates and reforms itself. Moreover, in a society where every child is to be treated as an end in himself rather than an object to be used and exploited, the child's own needs, interests, capacities, and aspirations should occupy a central place in education.

FACULTY PSYCHOLOGY

From the fact that man reasons, recalls, and imagines, faculty psychologists erroneously inferred that there must be a single entity which is causally responsible for man's varied mental functions. This entity called *the mind* was assumed to have different powers or faculties. By now it should be clear that the concept of faculty has no empirical basis other than man's everyday experience of reasoning, imagining, recalling, etc. But the fact that man performs a variety of mental activities does not necessarily imply that there is an entity which causes man to carry out these functions. Like other empiricists, Thorndike found the notion of *faculty* to be empirically untenable and meaningless. In his own words:

> The opinion that attention, memory, reasoning, choice and the like are mystical powers given to man as his birth right which weigh the dice in favor of thinking or doing one thing rather than another . . . is vanishing from the world of expert thought and no more need to be said about it than that it is false and would be useless to human welfare if true.[55]

Faculty psychology as an objective science of the mind based on exact observation should give scientifically verifiable explanations. Yet, the notion of faculty, having no empirical grounds, is neither verifiable nor refutable in any

55. Thorndike, *Educational Psychology*, Vol. II, p. 73.

scientific sense. That is, it is impossible to determine whether the claims of faculty psychologists are true or false on objective grounds. And therefore, at best, the explanatory powers of their claims are suspect. As other psychologists have shown, human behavior can be explained, predicted, and controlled with reasonable precision and success without the use of a concept such as *faculty*. In short, the term *faculty* is unnecessary in explaining man's behavior and therefore, by assuming it, faculty psychologists have violated the principle of parsimony, also known as Occam's Razor. In brief, this principle states that entities should not be multiplied beyond necessity and that, of the available explanations, the simplest should be adopted. This principle is based on the assumption that nature itself "prefers" simplicity, and hence by adopting the simplest explanation we can get closer to the nature of reality. It implies that if we can explain man's mental activities without presupposing the existence of a substantial mind, we should not assume that such an entity exists. Thus, faculty psychologists have not only failed to give adequate empirical explanations as to how man's mental functions are carried out but they have also introduced an additional problem of explaining the nature of the faculty and how it causally influences our bodily actions.

THE SUBSTANTIVE VIEW OF MIND

In spite of the many serious objections which have been raised against the substantive view, historically it is one of the most influential and widely held concepts of the mind in the West. Certainly this position is consistent with and congenial to the Christian view of man as possessing a mind distinct from the body. Accordingly, man's mind, being a separate entity, is believed to survive physical death. Thus immortality of the soul is made possible. Furthermore, since the mind was said to be the agent which animates the body and unifies human experience, it was thought to be superior to the body. This meant that man's spiritual and intellectual activities were more sublime and more valuable than his physical and sensual aspects. Some historians suggest that it is this dualism that enabled Descartes to continue his physiological study of the human body and animal vivisections without being condemned as a heretic by the Church. Even today the substantive view appeals to most laymen, who believe that they have "something" which is responsible for thinking, reasoning, willing, and making moral judgments. The suggestion that such a nonphysical entity is not empirically verifiable does not disturb them. But many readily agree that what is inconceivable to man may indeed be true, and from this they often erroneously conclude that therefore what we do not see or understand must be true. For example, "you cannot prove that God doesn't exist, therefore, He does exist."

As some readers may have noted, the substantive view is not only a theory about the human mind but it is also a philosophical basis upon which the formal discipline theory of teaching and faculty psychology rests. Hence, if the existence of substantial mind is either refuted or shown to be meaningless, neither doctrine can stand its ground. However, this does not necessarily imply that such mental exercises as drilling, reciting, and memorizing are invalid methods of teaching, for they can be defended and justified on other psychological or pedagogical grounds. Yet, it would be sheer nonsense to talk about them as means of strengthening the faculties if the mind as a nonextended substance possessing various mental powers is shown to be false and impossible.

In defending the substantive view, three able contemporary philosophers, Broad, Ducasse, and Ewing, argue that the objections raised by their opponents are not sufficient to refute the doctrine of substantial mind. Yet, they have not given us any positive grounds demonstrating the validity of their dualistic position. While it is true that what we cannot explain or understand is not necessarily false just because we can neither explain nor understand it, what is unexplainable is not true simply because it is unexplainable. Even if we agree with Broad and the others, the insufficiency of their critics' objections does not establish the validity of the substantive view. It would not help dualists to avoid the dilemma of asserting the existence of a unique and mysterious kind of mind-body causation without being able to explain how such a special sort of relation is possible, for neither minds nor bodies are said to share any characteristics which are relevant to mind-body interaction. One way of avoiding the interactionist difficulty is to deny that mind and body are distinct entities and to regard them as either two different aspects of a single substance or as different ways of talking about the various dimensions of one entity or process. In brief, we may escape from the interactionist dilemma by rejecting dualism and assuming a monistic view of the mind. In the following chapters we will examine several major monistic concepts of the mind as they relate to teaching and learning theories.

BIBLIOGRAPHY

Books

Adler, Mortimer J., "In Defense of the Philosophy of Education," *Philosophies of Education*, Nelson B. Henry, ed., Forty First Yearbook of NSSE. Chicago: University of Chicago Press, 1942.

———— *What Man Has Made of Man.* New York: Frederick Ungar Publishing Co., 1937.

Anable, Raymond J., *Philosophical Psychology.* New York: Fordham University Press, 1950.

Berelson, Bernard, and Gary A. Steiner, *Human Behavior: An Inventory of Scientific Findings.* New York: Harcourt, Brace & World, Inc., 1964.

Bode, Boyd Henry, *How We Learn.* New York: D. C. Heath and Co., 1940.

Broad, C. D., *The Mind and Its Place in Nature.* Totowa, N. J.: Littlefield, Adams & Co., 1960.

Ducasse, Curt, "In Defense of Dualism," *Dimensions of Mind*, Sidney Hook, ed. New York: New York University Press, 1960.

Eaton, Ralph M., *Descartes Selections.* New York: Charles Scribner's Sons, 1927.

Ewing, A. C., *Non-Linguistic Philosophy.* New York: Humanities Press, 1968.

Hutchins, Robert M., *The Higher Learning in America.* New Haven: Yale University Press, 1936.

Porter, Noah, *The Human Intellect.* New York: Charles Scribner's Sons, 1883.

Ryle, Gilbert, *The Concept of Mind.* London: Hutchinson & Co., 1949.

Thorndike, Edward L., *Educational Psychology,* Vol. II, *Psychology of Learning.* New York: Teachers' College, Columbia University, 1913.

Walker, James, ed., *Reid's Essays on Intellectual Powers of Man.* Cambridge: John Bartlett, 1850.

White, Emerson E., *The Art of Teaching.* New York: American Book Company, 1901.

Periodicals

Hyram, George H., "An Experiment in Developing Critical Thinking in Children." *Journal of Experimental Education,* December, 1957.

Skelton, Robert B., "High School Foreign Language Study and Freshman Performance." *School and Society,* June 8, 1957.

3

The Apperception Theory of Teaching, Structuralism, and the Bundle-Theory of Mind

THE APPERCEPTION THEORY OF TEACHING

Historically, the apperception theory of teaching was an integral part of Herbartianism, which contributed much toward making the study of education empirical. As a theory of education, Herbartianism was concerned with both psychological and moral dimensions of education, of which teaching was one important aspect. The apperception theory of teaching, also known as the Herbartian theory, was originally formulated by the nineteenth-century educational philosopher and psychologist, Johann Friedrich Herbart (1776–1841), and revised by his followers.[1] In brief, the theory asserts that new experiences and facts are learned and made a permanent part of the mind by incorporating them with the learner's previously acquired knowledge and experience. In this country Herbartianism dominated teachers' education as late as the mid-1920s.[2] Today we seldom meet anyone who explicitly advocates Herbartianism, but we still find aspects of teaching in our schools, colleges, and universities reflecting the general patterns suggested by the apperception theory of teaching. For example, there are many teachers who not only

1. Two of Herbart's better known European followers were Tuiskon Ziller and Wilhelm Rein. In America, Charles and Frank McMurry, Karl Colkmar Stoy, Charles De Garmo, and Alexis F. Lange were Herbartians.
2. In his book *Herbart and Education* (p. 124) Harold B. Dunkel indicates that Charles McMurry's *The Elements of General Method* was reprinted as late as 1923, after selling about 70,000 copies. *The Method of the Recitation* by C. A. and F. M. McMurry was revised in 1923 also and sold about 23,000 copies. De Garmo's *Essentials of Method* was in print as late as 1934 and sold about 33,000 copies.

adhere to rather rigidly fixed lesson plans but also see the learner as having a passive role in the teaching-learning process.

Aims of Teaching

As was pointed out earlier, the apperception theory of instruction was not merely a body of recipe-like "how to" suggestions about teaching, but was an indispensable part of a systematic and comprehensive Herbartian science of education, i.e., *pedagogics,* which consisted of "government" *(Regierung),* "discipline" *(Zucht),* and "instruction" *(Unterricht).* These three divisions represented a variety of interrelated activities through which the teacher was to realize the fundamental objective of education to make every child moral. All instructional materials and procedures were to be evaluated and selected in terms of their contribution toward achieving this end, because building moral character is "like a loadstone, attracting and subordinating all other purposes to itself. It should dominate in the choice, arrangement, and method of studies."[3] In short, the *pedagogics* had both ethical and psychological bases, the former pointing out the goal of education and the latter giving us the means of achieving it.

While "government" and "discipline" were important because they controlled children's behavior and showed them how the will should act in making moral judgments, "instruction" was the dominant and the most complex of the three divisions. The Herbartian theory of instruction was founded on the psychological premise that the content of the mind, the feelings and desires as well as the meanings of human experiences, is determined by presentations (new experiences) and the way in which such experiences are incorporated into and associated with what has already been acquired and is enduring in the learner's mind. Consequently, the degree to which we can influence and control the nature of the

---

3. Charles A. McMurry, *The Elements of General Method,* p. 7.

mind and the character of the child depends heavily upon our ability to control presentations. And since teaching means presenting something new to the child's attention, the Herbartian teachers became primarily interested in the nature of instructional materials and the order of presentation which would result in the most effective and efficient assimilation of newly learned material. Thus, the purpose of instruction was conceived as giving proper direction to the thoughts and impulses of the learner and stimulating all that is best in him. In other words, teaching should arouse *many-sided interest,* i.e., a balanced intellectual activity in which the learner's attention is directed toward many different kinds of interests without having any one of them dominate the child's effort. In Herbart's own words: "The business of instruction is to form the person on many sides, and accordingly to avoid a distracting dissipating effect. And instruction has successfully avoided this in the case of one who with ease surveys his well-arranged knowledge *in all of its unifying relations* and holds it together as his *very own.*"[4] This means that many-sided interests aroused by teaching are only a means to an end, viz., the unity of self or self-consciousness leading to the development of moral character.

For Herbartians, *interest* implies self-activity, and therefore, asking for many-sided interests is asking for many-sided self-activities. But this does not mean that any and all self-activities are educationally desirable. Herbart pointed out that we ought to seek only the right degrees of the right kinds of interests. And since there are many different sources and kinds of interests, it is necessary to find the criteria by which we can determine those interests that are educationally worthwhile. In his attempt to discover the right kind of interests, Herbart found that neither the quality of being interesting (superficially amusing) nor the nature of intellectual disciplines was adequate for his purpose. Moreover, since he regarded the mental faculties as fictions they too were of

4. John Frederick Herbart, *Outlines of Educational Doctrine*, p. 49.

little help in identifying the proper kinds of interest. Herbart finally concluded that the major sources of our interests lie in our experiences with objects and our associations with other human beings. In other words, educationally desirable interests can be grouped into two categories: (a) those interests arising from knowledge and (b) those which come from association with others. The knowledge interests were then subdivided into (1) empirical, (2) speculative, and (3) aesthetic interests, while the association interests were made up of (1) sympathetic, (2) social, and (3) religious interests. In Herbart's own words:

> The empirical interest is the mental eagerness aroused by direct appeal to the senses. . . . Speculative interest rests on perception of the relations of cause and effect. . . . Aesthetic interest rests on the enjoyment of contemplation.
>
> All of these interests, the empirical, the speculative, and the aesthetic, may be classed as *individual,* since they rest upon purely subjective grounds. . . . But the remaining groups, the sympathetic, the social, and the religious, rest upon the idea of intercourse with others. They are, therefore, of supreme importance for civilized life.[5]

Though this classification of interests is Herbart's own, most Herbartians accepted this scheme. They further agreed that teaching should link our experiences with objects and other human beings to avoid one-sided interest, because preoccupation with any single type of experience leads to unbalanced and stilted character.[6] For example, empirical interest can become one-sided if we study only one kind of object to the exclusion of others, while speculative interest becomes lopsided when we confine ourselves to metaphysical or logical matters alone. And again, aesthetic interest becomes narrow when we concentrate on painting and sculpture to the neglect of other forms. When a man is willing to live only with his social peers or only with fellow countrymen, sympathetic

5. *Ibid.,* p. 76.
6. *Ibid.,* pp. 81–82.

interest becomes one-sided. Herbart goes on to explain that social interest grows unbalanced when we give ourselves wholly to one political party and measure good or bad according to the success or failure of that party. Religious interest develops unevenly when we commit ourselves to one creed and view others as unworthy or false. In short, teaching should help the child to become a well-rounded, liberally educated person who is morally sound, open-minded, and tolerant of other views and people.

Presentative, Analytic, and Synthetic Instruction

As useful as the classification of interests is, by itself it could not give us an adequate guide for teaching. Herbartians needed to know much more about the process and the proper manner of instruction. According to Herbart and his followers, instruction can be *merely presentative, analytic, or synthetic. Merely presentative instruction* has to do with introducing to the learner those materials and activities which do not belong to what he has already acquired as a result of previous learning and experience. Since new materials and activities can extend the pupil's range of actual experience, it is important that the teacher master the skills of presenting the subject matter in a vivid and stimulating way. And,

> if the presentation has been a success, the reproduction by the pupils will show that they recall, not merely the main facts, but largely even the teacher's language. They have retained more exactly than they have been asked to do. Besides, the teacher who narrates and describes well gains a strong hold on the affections of his pupils; he will find them more obedient in matters pertaining to discipline.[7]

Analytic instruction, on the other hand, analyzes the various components of what the learner already knows. Children become familiar with many things through their experience,

---

7. *Ibid.,* p. 109.

but experience by itself does not give the child organized knowledge, because the child's experiences, as he undergoes them, are unstructured masses of things and events, and therefore, "it becomes the task of instruction to reverse this order and adjust the facts of experience to the sequence demanded by teaching."[8] This means "every thoughtful teacher [should be] led by his healthy act to analyse the masses which accumulate in children's brains, which are increased by merely descriptive instruction, and he must concentrate attention such cessively [Sic.] on the little and the least, to secure clearness and transparency in all presentations."[9]

In *synthetic instruction* the most important task is to help students secure a comprehensive view of whatever they are studying by seeing a familiar whole as a part of a larger whole. For example, children can be aided to see man as not only a mammal but also a member of the animal kingdom, as not only a member of a family but also as a member of the larger society in which he lives. Thus students are guided through synthetic instruction to assimilate and organize their new knowledge and also to understand a whole in terms of its parts and that whole in terms of a still larger whole. Hence, "synthetic instruction, which builds with its own stones, is alone capable of erecting the entire structure of thought which education requires."[10]

According to the apperception theory, teaching must always point out the new and assimilate it with the old, and then apply what has been learned to new situations. That is, teaching must have (1) clarity, (2) association, (3) system, and (4) method.[11] By clarity is meant that the child should not be confused by inappropriate and vague presentations of a subject, but that he should be able to understand the material thoroughly. Once the material is presented to the child clearly,

8. *Ibid.*, pp. 110–111.
9. Johann Friedrich Herbart, *The Science of Education*, p. 155.
10. *Ibid.*, p. 158.
11. Herbart, *Outlines of Educational Doctrine*, pp. 53–54.

the new must be related to the knowledge which is already in his mind. To put it differently, the new subject must be incorporated into the child's *apperceptive masses*. Once the new learning becomes assimilated with past learning, it should be organized into a more *systematic* and comprehensive order. In this way new learning takes on deeper meaning, while the past learning acquires a broader and enriched significance. Finally, the result of this learning process, a new apperceptive mass, should be *methodically* applied to the practical situations in the learner's life. By the use of these four steps or levels of approach to teaching, Herbart hoped to provide unified and coherent teaching to facilitate the most effective and efficient learning. In examining the rationale for these four steps we find that they are based on the belief that effective assimilation of new learning with the old requires acts of absorption *(Vertiefung)* and reflection *(Besinnung)*.[12] In the act of absorption the pupil concentrates on an object or a concept exclusively so that he can clearly understand its qualities and characteristics, while in reflection the learner systematically connects the new material to what he already knows without losing the clarity of understanding.

The Five Formal Steps

Though the Five Formal Steps have frequently been attributed to Herbart, they are actually elaborations of his four levels or modes of teaching by his followers. It is true that individual Herbartians followed a number of variations of the steps in their teaching, but they generally accepted Charles De Garmo's version. According to De Garmo the Five Steps were: 91) *Preparation,* (2) *Presentation,* (3) *Association,* (4) *Systematization* or *Generalization,* and (5) *Application*.[13] According to the Steps the teacher must first prepare the

12. Herbart, *Science of Education*, pp. 123–126.
13. Herbart, *Outlines of Educational Doctrine*, p. 59. For a similar discussion of the Steps refer to *The Method of the Recitation* by C. A. and F. M. McMurry, pp. 288–328.

learner's mind by helping him to remember certain aspects of knowledge and experience he already possesses. This first step is essentially analytic in that the store of knowledge and experience is analyzed to bring certain facts to the fore, so that they can be related to the new lesson. In the next step new facts are presented so that they become connected to that with which the learner is already acquainted. This second step is primarily synthetic since its function is to add the material of a new lesson to previously acquired knowledge. Freshly learned facts are then incorporated into the apperceptive masses in the third step to enrich and enlarge the learner's experience. In the fourth step, generalizations are developed on the basis of new and old knowledge to show how they belong to a common principle or fact. These generalizations are then applied to new situations in the last step to explain further facts thereby making new facts permanent. For example, in teaching about energy we might begin by reminding our children of the changes brought about by various forms of natural forces such as tornados, floods, and earthquakes. This preparation can be followed with a presentation of new facts about energy. Here we can explain to children that things like heat, electricity, and light are different kinds of things from matter in that they neither have mass nor occupy space. Energy then can be presented as "what makes matter change." This concept may be further illustrated by demonstrating how a warm pot is different from a cold pot because of heat, or how electricity operates motors of various kinds, or how a lamp gives off light. In the third step we can discuss the ways in which heat, electric, and light energies are associated with changing water from liquid to solid, or from liquid to gas, the fading of the dye in our clothes, and the operation of electrical appliances. These facts can now be systematized and generalized in the fourth step to show that forces coming from tornados, floods, earthquakes, heat, electricity, and light are all different forms of atomic energy. In the fifth and last step the concept of energy may be elaborated and applied to explain such other forms as chemical, mechanical, and kinetic energies. These steps can of course be used to teach lessons on democracy and other similar concepts and principles. Though these Formal Steps may appear anachronistic, they are not completely alien to us, for we still have many teachers who faithfully follow a fixed set of teaching procedures which conform to the basic principles of the Herbartian Steps.

Apperception

The Five Formal Steps we have just discussed are based on the premise that human experiences are the results of "interaction" between new perceptions and previous experiences. In other words, previous experiences do not drop out of our minds but remain in the subconscious as a background against which new experiences are seen. While the earlier experiences leave the focal point of our attention they continue to add color and dimension to our experience and knowledge. Hence, "the old ideas dwelling in the mind are not to be regarded as dead treasures stored away and occasionally drawn out and used by a purposed effort of the memory, but they are living forces which have the active power of seizing and appropriating new ideas."[14] According to the theory of apperception, not only is the meaning of new thought to be understood with the help of past experiences, but the quality and strength of our new emotions and volitions are dependent on the qualities and strength of old emotions and volitions. To Alexis F. Lange, a nineteenth-century American Herbartian, apperception was the "interaction between two similar ideas or thought-complexes in the course of which the weaker, unorganized, isolated idea or thought-complex is incorporated into the richer, better digested, and more firmly compacted one."[15]

This implies that one of the primary tasks of the teacher

14. McMurry, *General Method*, p. 259.
15. *Ibid.*, p. 263.

should be to know what objects ought to be presented to the child in what way and in what order so that the child can appropriately incorporate recent learning with the apperceptive masses. Hence, the teacher must have the skills necessary to make clear and effective presentations of instructional materials and also to be aware of what knowledge and experiences are already possessed by the child, because "the capacity for education [learning] . . . is determined not by the faculties' stand to one another, but by the relations of ideas already acquired to one another."[16] This means the presentation of new materials must begin with what is already familiar and interesting to the child rather than follow the logical order in which the subject matter is organized. For example, in teaching biology it is important to begin with those living things which are familiar to the learner. We should not rigidly conform to a logical scheme of biological nomenclature, e.g., classification of the animal kingdom beginning with protozoans and ending with vertebrates, because emphasis on the logical sequence of a discipline is likely to lead to the kind of teaching in which subject matter becomes the central concern. When teaching is thought of as primarily a process of imparting information or carrying out mental exercises, facts and skills are usually thought of as separate things to be learned and only by coincidence do the newly learned materials become connected with the old. Or as Herbart points out, "instruction in the sense of mere information-giving contains no guarantee whatever that it will materially counteract faults and influence existing groups of ideas that are independent of the imparted information."[17] Unlike the formal disciplinarians, the Herbartian teacher considers his understanding of the child's interests and the store of knowledge the child already has as central to teaching because effective teachers must know how to organize the child's mental resources, i.e., apperceptive masses, so that new experiences can be assimi-

16. Herbart, *Outlines of Educational Doctrine*, p. 21.
17. *Ibid.*, p. 23.

lated by them. Hence, the teacher must be concerned with helping the child retain what he has been taught by relating new lessons to what he already knows and also by maintaining a high level of interest in the child. It is important to note here that the advocates of the apperceptive theory viewed interest as the propensity of old ideas to become associated with similar new ideas. Hence, interest is a function of ideas and it arises from a vivid presentation of ideas that are capable of remaining in the learner's consciousness. This means that *interest* is more than a quality of being amusing. We must also remember that the proponents of the apperception theory used *interest* in two different senses. On the one hand they saw *interest* as the outcome of teaching and as such it referred to the pleasing feeling that came from the association of old and new ideas. On the other hand, *interest* was regarded as the means by which the apperceptive masses became connected with new ideas and experiences.

There are other important pedagogical implications that Herbartians drew from the general theory of apperception.[18] Namely, since acquired knowledge is important in learning new facts it should be constantly worked over and reviewed to keep it from being forgotten. In addition, children must be made to encounter new knowledge and to relate it to what they already know. This suggests that the teacher must help the child to unify his knowledge by giving him new materials and reviewing old ideas in the child's mind. To do this the teacher must know the child's store of knowledge, his experiences as well as his interests. For sound education it is essential that ideas learned at school are related to "home-bred" ideas. Education fails when we become preoccupied with school studies and ignore the rich fund of ideas that children bring from their homes, because this approach to education considers only a portion of the learner's experience. The teacher must then help the child to apply what he has learned and constantly to develop and refine his ideas so

18. McMurry, *General Method*, pp. 280–287, 290–292.

that they become clearer, enriched, and broadened. As McMurry points out, "apperception is the practical key to the most important problems of education, because it compels us to keep a sympathetic eye upon the child in his moods, mental states, and changing phases of growth; to build hourly upon the only foundation he has, his previous acquirements and habits."[19] It is no wonder that the Herbartian theory of teaching has been called the apperception theory of teaching.

Laws of Teaching

The apperception theory of teaching contains a number of laws or what Charles and Frank McMurry call "statements of a uniform sequence." They are laws of (1) *Induction*, (2) *Apperception*, (3) *Aim*, (4) *Self-activity*, (5) *Absorption* and *Reflection*, (6) *Motor Activity*, (7) *Interest*, and (8) *Correlation*.[20] The *law of induction* indicates that the acquisition of knowledge follows the same steps as the so-called scientific method involving observation of facts, comparison and classification of the observed, deduction of generalizations from the observed, and verification of hypothesis. The *law of apperception* tells us that new thoughts can be understood only by the help of old thoughts. According to the *law of aim*, definite and attractive aim is an essential condition for effective work of any kind, and the proper development of the learner is possible only through a high degree of self-activity, i.e., by conforming to the *law of self-activity*. The *law of absorption* and *reflection* suggests that we regularly alternate between absorption in details and reflection for effective thinking, while the *law of motor activity* points out that ideas must be expressed and realized in action prior to their clear and accurate conception. Lastly, the *laws of interest* and *correlation* indicate that the arousal of a deep interest in thoughts is necessary for them to have strong influence upon

19. *Ibid.*, p. 331.
20. McMurry and McMurry, *The Method of the Recitation*, pp. 288–296.

the character and mental life of the learner, whereas the educational worth of facts or instructional materials is determined not only by the clarity and accuracy with which they are conceived but also by how closely and widely they can be related to that which endures in the learner's mind.

In the history of education, the apperception theory of teaching represents the first earnest effort to apply empirical psychology to teaching. Regardless of how outdated the apperception theory may seem to us today, Herbartians did much to point out the vital role of the learner, his background, and his interests in the teaching-learning process. By conceiving the learning process in terms of apperception and also by promoting the integration of fragmented knowledge and perspectives of the learner, Herbartians successfully discredited the barren formalism of the formal discipline theory of teaching. In brief, advocates of the apperception theory emphatically insisted on the centrality of the pupil and the continuity of experience in education. The following words of Herbart concisely summarize the main thrust of the apperception theory:

> Instruction is to supplement that which has been gained already by experience and by intercourse with others; these foundations must exist when instruction begins. If they are wanting, they must be firmly established first. Any deficiency here means a loss to instruction, because the pupils lack the thoughts which they need in order to interpret the words of the teacher.
>
> In the same way, knowledge derived from earlier lessons must be extended and deepened by subsequent instruction. This presupposes such an organization of the whole work of instruction that that which comes later shall always find present the earlier knowledge with which it is to be united.
>
> In the most favorable case, if instruction is thorough, i.e., scientific, a foundation of elementary knowledge is gradually laid sufficiently solid for later years to build on; in other words, out of the elementary knowledge an apperceiving mass is created in the mind of the pupil which will aid him in his future studies.[21]

21. Herbart, *Outlines of Educational Doctrine*, pp. 69–70.

STRUCTURAL PSYCHOLOGY

Structuralism and the Apperception Theory

The apperception theory of teaching was originally based on Herbart's psychology of apperception. But in the nineteenth and early twentieth centuries much of its psychological justification came from the theoretical insights and empirical findings of structural psychology, the primary concern of which was to analyze and understand the structure of man's conscious mental states. Hence, a discussion of structuralism is most appropriate in examining the psychological basis of the apperception theory of teaching. Herbartians in general said very little about the relationship between their outlook and structural psychology, but both Karl Lange and Charles De Garmo, influential Herbartians in Europe and America respectively, referred to the works of an early structuralist, Wilhelm Wundt (1832–1920), as the major source of their views on apperception. Moreover, a comparison of the Herbartian and structuralist accounts of experience, learning, and apperception will give us additional clues to the close and organic kinship between these two pedagogical and psychological perspectives. In addition, in spite of his allegiance to the substantive view of mind, even Herbart's own psychology contained more than faint traces of early structuralism and associationistic psychology, for he argued that complex mental states are reducible to elementary sensory qualities which become connected to each other by certain laws of association. Wundt expressed a similar belief when he wrote:

> Closely related to Hume's psychological associationism is the psychology of Herbart. Herbart's doctrine of the statics and mechanics of ideas is a purely intellectualistic doctrine. (Feeling and volition are here recognized only as certain phases of ideas.) It is in an agreement with associationism in its fundamental mechanical view of mental life. This similarity is not to be overlooked merely because Herbart sought through certain hypothetical assumptions to give his psychological discussions an

exact mathematical form. There are many anticipations of voluntaristic psychology in the works of psychologists of the "pure introspection" school; and of the association schools. The first thorough-going exposition of this form of psychology was the work of the author of this *Outlines of Psychology* [Wundt's own work] in his psychological treatises. . . . Psychological voluntarism . . . looks upon empirical volitional processes with their constituent feelings, sensations, and ideas, as the types of all conscious processes. For such a voluntarism even volition is a complex phenomenon which owes its typical significance to this very fact that it includes in itself the different kinds of psychical elements.[22]

Structuralism as a science of mind was to study human consciousness by following the same procedures employed by the natural sciences. Both Wundt and Edward B. Titchener (1867–1927), an American structuralist, insisted that since the methods of physical sciences consisted of analyzing a substance into its irreducible units and then studying their interrelations, psychology too must begin by first analyzing the structure of man's consciousness into its most elementary processes and then examine the relationship between them. Structuralists argued that by studying these elementary mental processes they can formulate certain laws which govern the ways in which conscious states are formed. As Titchener explained:

The psychologist seeks, first of all, to analyze mental experience into its simplest components. He takes a particular consciousness and works over it again and again, phase by phase and process by process, until his process can go no further. He is left with certain mental processes which resist analysis, which are absolutely simple in nature, which cannot be reduced, even in part, to other processes. Then he proceeds to the task of synthesis. . . . He thus learns to formulate laws of connection of the elementary mental processes.[23]

22. Wilhelm Wundt, *Outlines of Psychology*, Charles Hubbard Judd, trans., pp. 19–20.
23. Edward B. Titchener, *Textbook of Psychology*, pp. 37–38.

According to structuralists, *mind,* which is the subject matter of psychology, is the sum-total of man's conscious experience and therefore, the content and structure of consciousness are directly accessible only to the person himself via introspection. Realizing the problems inherent in situations where the observed and the observer are one and the same, Titchener insisted that psychologists receive extensive laboratory training so that they could observe and analyze their own conscious states in an objective and systematic manner. Because structuralists were primarily interested in analyzing human consciousness in terms of certain irreducible mental processes, they were most concerned with experimental studies dealing with sensory processes. It is in this sense that they are often referred to as the first experimental psychologists.

Structuralism on Learning

As was suggested earlier, Herbartian educators concur with structural psychologists that learning occurs as a result of associations of various impressions, images, and feelings, with each other and also with what is already in the pupil's conscious mind. Associations of these elementary processes are then governed by laws of similarity, contrast, and contiguity. In other words, objects and ideas become connected with other objects and ideas when there is similarity or contrast between them. We also relate one set of events with another when they happen in close proximity in time and space, i.e., contiguously. Hence, when we see a flash of lightning we expect to hear a thunderclap, and when we see traffic lights we anticipate the usual red-green succession. These associations and anticipations are influenced by our previous encounters with objects, ideas, and events which are related to each other by similarity, contrast, and contiguity. In other words, "whenever a sensory or imaginal process occurs in consciousness, there are likely to appear with it (of course, in imaginal terms) all those sensory and imaginal processes which occurred together with it in any earlier conscious present. This we may term the law of association."[24] For Titchener, the sensory processes without contiguity (either spatial or temporal) similarity, and contrast were not sufficient to make associations occur between objects, ideas, or events. Therefore, Titchener reduced the three laws of association to a single law of contiguity.

In general, what structuralists had to say about learning is not anything like the contemporary accounts of the learning process. There were no experiments on either human or animal learning, because structuralists were concerned with learning only as a means of analyzing and understanding the ways in which man's conscious states are formed. Hence, much of the structuralist view on learning has to be inferred from their discussions of the laws of association, memory, and retention. It is interesting to note here that the three laws of association, viz., the laws of similarity, contrast, and contiguity, were first given by Aristotle as the laws of memory. They were then later restated by Thomas Hobbes, a seventeenth-century English philosopher, who reduced them to a single law of contiguity for very much the same reasons as Titchener's.

In analyzing mental states Titchener found that not all areas of man's consciousness have equal degrees of clarity. On the contrary, our conscious state has a number of regions with varying degrees of clarity. These regions are focus, margin, foreground and background, and center and periphery.[25] Focus has the greatest clarity and it is that with which we are presently occupied and to which we directly attend. The territories outside of the focus have different degrees of clarity which eventually shade off to complete obscurity, i.e., below the threshold of consciousness. Yet, the importance of marginal areas cannot be ignored, for ideas and impulses from

24. *Ibid.*, p. 378.
25. *Ibid.*, pp. 266–268.

these areas often come into consciousness to influence the meaning of our experience and the content of our mind. That is, the meaning of elementary mental processes such as sensations, images, and feelings is determined by the context to which the marginal areas belong. Hence, the meaning of our experiences comes from our current sensory processes as well as from the rest of our past experiences. As Titchener pointed out, simple sensations by themselves do not have any meaning, because

> meaning, psychologically, is always context; one mental process is the meaning of another mental process if it is that other's context. And context, in this sense, is simply the mental process which accrues to the given process through the situation in which the organism finds itself. Originally, the situation is physical, external; and, originally, meaning is kinaesthesis; the organism faces the situation by some bodily attitude, and the characteristic sensations which the attitude arouses give meaning to the process which stands at the conscious focus, are psychologically the meaning of the process.[26]

Pedagogically, Titchener's conclusion suggests that effective teaching must take into account not only the nature of instructional materials and methods but also the pupil's background, knowledge, and interest in facilitating conditions for desired learning to occur.

Attention   In terms of what has been said about human consciousness and its various regions, it is essential that appropriate sensory experiences and mental images be brought to the foreground for learning. We must *attend* to that which we are about to learn. *Attention* then is nothing more than clarity. It is a form of conscious state in which certain sensory experiences acquire clarity. In other words, the elementary sensations gain intensity and prominence in their associations as they go through various stages of the development of attention. There are three general stages through

26. *Ibid.*, p. 367.

which attention develops. They are: (1) *primary attention,* (2) *secondary attention,* and (3) *derived primary attention.*[27] *Primary attention* is the response we give to certain stimuli either voluntarily or involuntarily. We often choose to attend to an idea or an object. On the other hand, we are frequently "compelled" to respond to intensive stimuli. For example, we can willingly and deliberately decide to reflect about the nature of moral good or the concept of liberal education. But we react involuntarily to an unexpected explosion or a flash of bright light in our eyes. We inescapably notice the repetitious sounds coming from a phonograph record with the needle stuck between the grooves or a sudden change in temperature. We are often attracted to graceful motions of birds, or to a beautiful sunset, or to events that are strikingly similar to our previous experience. In brief, our attention is determined by such factors as intensity, repetition, suddenness, movement, novelty, and congruity, which all elementary mental processes possess in varying degrees.[28] *Secondary attention* is the stage in which we consciously and deliberately direct our attention to an object or a thought although we are attracted (distracted) by other things. We may be tempted to watch a television program, but we force ourselves to concentrate on a problem in mathematics. If we persist and win over the temptation, we become absorbed and interested in the problem, which will eventually acquire the same forceful hold over us as a stimulating television program would. This involuntary absorption or attention comes in the third or *derived primary stage,* in which we attend to the problem by overcoming opposition or competing stimuli (temptations and distractions). That is, we become so completely occupied with solving our mathematical problem that we are neither concerned with nor interested in other activities.

These three stages are not discrete and separate, but are continuous conditions. An example of this continuity is the

27. *Ibid.,* p. 275.
28. *Ibid.,* pp. 268–269.

development of interest in reading. For instance, in reading a philosophical book our attention may be held by novelty in the beginning. As reading progresses the novelty wears off and certain inhibitory factors may develop. Encounters with new and abstruse terms and involved expositions distract us from reading. Frequently, academic difficulties faced by students are attributed to their inability to overcome inhibitory factors. But if we persist and continue to "fight" against the distractions we may find ourselves becoming more and more engrossed in the material. "Looking at life in the large, we may say that the period of training or education is a period of secondary attention, and that following the period of achievement and mastery is a period of derived primary attention. Looking at experience in more detail, we see that education itself consists, psychologically, in alternation of the two attentions: habit is made the basis of further acquisition, and acquisition—gained with pains—passes in its turn into habit; the circle recurs, so long as the organism retains its nervous plasticity."[29]

Attention and Apperception   The centrality of attention to apperception is indicated in Herbart's statement that "we attend for the sake of the apperception of the object, which, left to itself, would have been forgotten."[30] And as Gardner Murphy summarizes, apperception is "the process by which the elements of experience are appropriated or laid hold of by the individual; that is, drawn into clear introspective consciousness."[31] Through apperception such elementary processes as sensations, images, and feelings become organized into a whole, which acquires its meaning in relation to the totality of present and past experiences. Hence, contents of the marginal areas of our consciousness and apperceptive

29. *Ibid.*, pp. 275–276.
30. Johann Friedrich Herbart, *The Application of Psychology to the Science of Education,* Beatrice C. Mulliner, trans., p. 209.
31. Gardner Murphy, *Historical Introduction to Modern Psychology,* pp. 153–154.

masses are important, because they give meaning to present perceptions. But apperception could not take place without a clear grasp of that with which we are presently occupied. In short, apperception occurs at the focal point of attention. In the following metaphor Herbart illustrates the importance of attention in one type of learning: "Here consciousness presents itself to us as a plain whereon grow certain little plants; high mountains and deep rivers should not be near them, unless a new energy, voluntary attention . . . comes to the assistance of reproduction."[32] To put this another way, when our attempt to memorize certain facts is hindered by the presence of stronger impressions, we need the energy of voluntary attention to make memorization successful. Apperception then occurs neither automatically nor passively, for it is always accompanied by a conscious feeling of self-activity and the excitement of discovery, which comes when we attain a clear grasp of the meaning of perceptual situations in their proper contexts.

By now it should be clear that the concept of attention is essential to the apperception theory and also to the structuralist view of learning. Although the term apperception was discarded by Titchener and his contemporaries, many aspects of Herbart's doctrine of apperception remained as important parts of the concept of attention.

Structuralists on Mind

Fundamentally, the structuralist account of learning is founded on an analysis of the process of apperception and the laws of association, which govern the ways in which various elementary sensations combine to form complex mental states. Philosophically, this concept of learning is rooted in the belief that mind, the subject matter of psychology, is "the sum-total of mental processes occuring in the life-time of an

---

32. Herbart, *Application of Psychology*, p. 219.

individual."[33] Thus, *mind* is nothing more than the sum of inner experiences, ideation, feeling, and willing, collected into a unified system in consciousness and "at no point in our explanation of the interconnection of these inner experiences have we found occasion to apply this attribute of mentality to anything else than the concrete complex of idea, feeling, and will."[34] Similarly, *self* is "simply and solely the perception of the interconnection of internal experiences which accompanies that experience itself."[35] Hence, Wundt and Titchener agree that mind and body are not two separate entities interacting with each other, because they are simply two aspects of the same world of experience. Mind and body cannot causally influence each other, for they are not two independent things. Mental processes do not cause physical processes or vice versa, but every mental state has a corresponding physical condition.[36] This is what the two structuralists call *psychophysical parallelism.* At first Wundt and Titchener may appear to be dualists because they argue for a type of parallelism which assigns two distinct and separate identities to mind and body, but a closer examination will show that their psychophysical parallelism is not dualistic in the same sense in which the doctrines of pre-established harmony and occasionalism (as discussed in Chapter 2) are.

What is puzzling about this structuralist stance is that at times Wundt and Titchener seem to be taking mind and body as two different aspects of a single substance, but at other times they appear to imply that the mental and the physical are simply two different ways of talking about one and the same process. And at still other times they write as if mind and body are two independent processes. For example, in the following excerpt Titchener states that mental states, e.g.,

33. Titchener, *Psychology,* p. 19.
34. Wilhelm Wundt, *Lectures on Human and Animal Psychology,* J. E. Creighton and E. B. Titchener, trans., p. 451.
35. *Ibid.,* p. 250.
36. *Ibid.,* pp. 364–365.

grief or remorse, exist completely apart from any physical stimuli in our nervous system:

> If we look at the whole experience under its independent aspect, we find that certain physical events, certain stimuli, affect the body; they set up in the body, and especially in the nervous system, certain physical changes; these changes cause the secretion of tears. This is an exhaustive account of the experience, considered as independent of the experiencing person. If we look at the experience under its dependent aspect, we find that our consciousness has been invaded by grief or remorse or some kindred emotion. The two sets of events, physical and mental, are parallel, but they do not interfere with each other.[37]

If physical and mental events are parallel, they cannot and do not causally affect each other. And if this were true, then we could conclude that only physical events can cause other physical events and only mental processes can make other mental processes occur. Yet Titchener tells us that we cannot regard one mental process as the cause of another.[38] For example, the cause of our consciousness of pain is not past consciousness but present stimuli, i.e., a physical event. But this asserts a causal connection between a physical and a mental event. If Titchener asserts that mental states are caused by physical states, then he is denying psychophysical parallelism, but if he remains consistent with his parallelism then he must admit that mental states can cause other mental states, unless he wishes to argue that mental events happen *ex nihilo,* i.e., from nothing, or to invoke the doctrines of pre-established harmony or occasionalism. In view of his empiricist temperament neither of these is a viable option for him. Titchener could, of course, regard the mental as an epiphenomenon, i.e., a by-product of the physical. But this would make the mental states completely contingent upon the existence of a body in the same manner in which shadows depend on bodies for their existence. It would seem that both Wundt and Titchener are obliged to conclude, as Hume did,

37. Titchener, *Psychology,* p. 14.
38. *Ibid.,* p. 39.

that the causes of mental events probably lie in the nervous system. Therefore, though we may not have precise knowledge about the causes of mental states, they must be physiological or physical in nature. But this conclusion makes Wundt and Titchener seem materialists, i.e., monists. We may indeed wonder if they were not trying to save thought and mental states from becoming mere epiphenomena by asserting psychophysical parallelism, for in this way they may have hoped to avoid materialism, which usually regards the mental and the physical as merely two different ways of talking about a single process, i.e., the physical process.

Although there seems to be little doubt that the Humean analysis of human experience into its constituent elementary sensations was perhaps the most important forerunner of structural psychology, neither Wundt nor Titchener explicitly indicated Hume's influence on their views. In a very important sense Wundt's concept of the mind, which is the foundation of his structuralism, is a psychologically refined version of Hume's bundle-theory of mind, because

> the reduction by Hume of soul or mind to a bundle of sensations and his doctrine that images are faint copies of sensations are illustrative of this shift [the English empiricists' shift of introspective interest from the area of higher mental processes to that of sensations]. Wundt continued this tendency toward simplicity by further refining the conscious elements and by combining the introspective process with experiment.[39]

Hume did not, as did Wundt and Titchener, maintain psychophysical parallelism between mind and body, but he did suggest that the causes of mental processes may be physical in nature.[40] As was pointed out earlier, it appears that both Wundt and Titchener would have to concede that mental states have physical causes, because if they cannot cause other mental states we are led to conclude that mental events are either caused by physical events or they are not caused at all. But the latter of these alternative positions is simply

---

39. R. I. Watson, *The Great Psychologists From Aristotle to Freud*, p. 243.
40. David Hume, *A Treatise of Human Nature*, p. 3.

unintelligible, for what does it mean to say that a mental event, say my wish to sing, happened from nothing? Unfortunately, whether Wundt and Titchener would have eventually admitted to physical causation of mental states and rejected their psychophysical parallelism is open to conjectures. In any event, there seems to be a direct philosophical tie between Hume's bundle-theory and the structuralists' concept of mind. The following discussion of the bundle-theory may help us to see how closely Hume's views are related to those of Wundt and Titchener.

THE BUNDLE-THEORY OF MIND

In examining his own consciousness for traces of the mind or self as a simple and unextended substance, Hume did not discover any spiritual substratum which unified his various mental processes. Quite to the contrary, he found that in the moments of self-consciousness he was always aware of some particular perceptions, e.g., hot, cold, or smooth, but never a simple sensation of a substantial mind. Hume wrote:

> For my part, when I enter most intimately into what I call *myself*, I always stumble on some particular perception or other, of heat or cold, light or shade, love or hatred, pain or pleasure. I never can catch myself at any time without a perception, and never can observe anything but the perception. When my perceptions are removed for any time, as by sound sleep, so long am I insensible of myself, and may truly be said not to exist. And were all my perceptions removed by death, and could I neither think, nor feel, nor see, nor love, nor hate, after the dissolution of my body, I should be entirely annihilated, nor do I conceive what is further requisite to make me a perfect nonentity.[41]

Hence, the self is not to be described as an entity but only as a bundle or collection of perceptions tied together by certain laws of association. Similarly, the mind is to be considered as

41. Hume, *Human Nature*, p. 239.

a system of different perceptions or a "kind of theatre, where several perceptions successively make their appearance; pass, repass, glide away, and mingle in an infinite variety of postures and situations."[42] This view is essentially the same as Wundt's notion that the mind is simply the perception of the interconnection of inner experiences[43] and Titchener's concept of mind as the sum-total of mental processes.[44] In the words of a more recent advocate of the Humean position, mind is "the group of mental events which form part of the history of a certain living body."[45] The term *mind* therefore does not stand for any "thing" or for a single principle of unity, nor does *self* represent a metaphysical substance. Consequently, the ideas and perceptions which become connected associate themselves independently of any specific purpose or action of the separate mind and apart from the truth or falsehood of the ideas themselves. If there is no single source of power unifying our perceptions, how can simple impressions and ideas combine to form complex impressions or ideas? Moreover, if impressions and ideas become associated with each other without the controlling mind, would their association not occur by chance and hence lack coherence? Hume points out that relations of resemblance, contiguity, and causality[46] make simple impressions and ideas cohere into a complex cognitive structure. It is not difficult to see that in our daily experience associations are more easily established among similar ideas, objects that are close to-

---

42. *Ibid.*, pp. 239–240.
43. Wundt, *Lectures on Psychology*, p. 250.
44. Titchener, *Psychology*, p. 16.
45. Bertrand Russell, *An Outline of Philosophy*, p. 286.
46. To Hume the statement "C causes E" means the same as "C is constantly followed by E." What distinguishes causality from temporal sequence is that the former contains the notion of necessary connection. That is, because of our previous experience of observing constant conjunction between events C and E, we believe that the occurrence of C must necessarily lead to the occurence of E. To put it differently, when we see C we anticipate E because of our habit of associating those events which occur in constant conjunction. Our idea of necessary connection does not come from a perception of a mysterious power (i.e., causality) or a metaphysical glue which is believed to connect events together. Hence, for Hume causality does not imply power but only constant conjunction of events.

gether, and events which occur in conjunction. It is important to remember that Hume is not denying unity or coherence in human experience, but objecting to the notion of self as representing a metaphysical substance which is believed to be the source of a single unifying force in man. As Norman Kemp Smith observes:

> His [Hume's] quarrel, therefore, with those who maintain a doctrine of personal identity is not in regard to the fact of there being a self or of its having, as a quite essential characteristic, a principle of *union,* but only with those who would interpret its varied, ever-changing complex features in terms of "identity." The self, alike in its variability and its complexity is . . . to be understood (so far as 'understanding' is humanly possible at all) solely in terms of relation.[47]

The self, then, is the feeling of smoothness in the transition from one perception to another as determined by relations of resemblance, contiguity, and causality, which constitute the principles of union or the laws of association.[48] But Hume cautions us that these laws establish inseparable connections between ideas and impressions, because associations depend on certain conditions which are not known to man.[49] In other words, we have no knowledge of the causes of associations. We only know that association as a "gentle force" occurs when there are no counteracting conditions. Hume insists that it would be unfruitful to speculate about the nature of the causes of association, because he is convinced that they are beyond the range of intelligible explanation. Consequently, Hume remarks that

> nothing is more requisite for a true philosopher, than to restrain the intemperate desire of searching into causes; and having established any doctrine upon a sufficient number of experiments, rest contented with that, when he sees a further examination would lead him into obscure and uncertain speculations. In that

47. Norman Kemp Smith, *The Philosophy of David Hume,* pp. 500–501.
48. Hume, *Human Nature,* p. 240.
49. *Ibid.,* p. 21.

case this inquiry would be much better employed in examining the effects than causes of his principle.[50]

Since any attempt to learn about the conditions which cause associations to occur according to the three laws will be useless we should be satisfied with the knowledge that associations do occur when there are resemblance, contiguity and causality. Yet curiously enough, Hume goes against his own advice by not only suggesting that mental processes may have physical causes but also by giving us the following physiological account of the causes of "many mistakes and sophisms in philosophy":

> I shall therefore observe, that as the mind is endowed with a power of exciting any idea it pleases; whenever it dispatches the spirits into that region of the brain, in which the idea is placed; these spirits always excite the idea, when they run precisely into the proper traces, and rummage that cell, which belongs to the idea. But as their motion is seldom direct, and naturally turns a little to the one side or the other; for this reason the animal spirits, falling into the contiguous traces, present other related ideas, in lieu of that which the mind desired at first to survey. This change we are not always sensible of; but continuing still the same train of thought, make use of the related idea, which is presented to us, and employ it in our reasoning, as if it were the same with what we demanded. This is the cause of many mistakes and sophisms in philosophy.[51]

As has been discussed, Hume's inquiry led him not to a simple self as an entity, but to a collection of perceptions. Therefore, he denied the substantial mind as the unifying agent of human experience. From this standpoint psychology was thought of as a means of dissecting and describing man's mental states by reducing them to elementary sensations which are combined and recombined according to the laws of association. Consequently, existence of the mind as an unextended substance was unnecessary in explaining man's mental

50. *Ibid.*
51. *Ibid.*, p. 65

functions, for they were describable in terms of the principles of association. In view of what has been discussed it should not be surprising that Wundt felt a close affinity with the psychological views of Hume and Herbart (see n. 22). Of course, Herbart did not subscribe to the Humean concept of the mind, for he postulated the substantial mind. But to Herbart as a psychologist this mind-substance was not as important as the process of apperception, because he was primarily interested in understanding the processes by which mental states are formed. In other words, Herbart's dualistic stand in regard to the mind-body problem was not essential to his pedagogical and psychological positions. Hence, it would seem entirely reasonable to agree with Bode's conclusion that

> Herbart was not quite ready to break completely with tradition, and so the substantive mind is retained, but is honorably retired on a pension. Or to change the figure of speech, the mind in Herbart's scheme occupies a status very much like that of a hereditary monarch in a country that is run by a system of popular government. Its position is one of considerable dignity but little power.[52]

CONCLUDING COMMENTS

THE APPERCEPTION THEORY OF TEACHING

Historically, the most significant pedagogical contribution made by the apperception theory of teaching is its repudiation of the barren doctrine of formal discipline by insisting that learning be viewed as a process by which new ideas and experiences become assimilated with and incorporated into what is already in the learner's mind. Thus, Herbartians pointed out the importance of interest, the child's background, and an enriched curriculum, and demanded that the teaching process commence at the point where the learner's

52. Boyd Henry Bode, *How We Learn*, pp. 151–152.

past experience and knowledge (the apperceptive masses) placed him. Further, they held that the development of teaching methods and procedures must be based on sound knowledge of man and an understanding of his mental functions. Herbartians were convinced that by adopting the apperceptive theory the teaching-learning process could not only be more effectively manipulated, but also that the outcome of curricular arrangements and even lesson plans could be brought within the limits of empirical control. Hence, under the influence of Herbart and his followers, educational psychology and pedagogy emerged as distinct and empirical disciplines. But strangely enough, the most influential and attractive aspects of the apperception theory later became targets for severe and frequent criticisms.

Unlike the formal disciplinarians who preceded them, Herbartians directed their attention to the role of interest in the teaching-learning process. They saw interest as a function of ideas and believed it came from the ability of old ideas and experiences to maintain themselves above the threshold of the learner's consciousness, thus becoming assimilated with new presentations to prevent other elements from appearing upon the scene. This meant the term *interest* was no longer understood as meaning superficially amusing qualities in ideas or activities; rather, it was understood to be an essential ingredient in learning. By conceiving interest as a function of ideas, the student was given a passive role. That is, the pupil was not regarded as actively involved in the learning process in which associations of ideas and impressions took place automatically. Herbartians did not regard interest as a self-propelling quality of life or as "the active or moving *identity* of the self with a certain object."[53] They did not see interest as the learner's attachment to an idea or object as a means of realizing the learner's purpose.

As Dewey pointed out, Herbartians took teaching out of routine and accident by making it a conscious business with a

---

53. John Dewey, *Democracy and Education*, p. 352.

definite aim and procedure within which everything could be specified.[54] However, they regarded learning as a process in which the pupil remained essentially passive, while the teacher was given the primary responsibility of organizing and presenting "right" materials in a "right" way so that the new could be properly incorporated into the old. Though the notion of relating newly learned materials with knowledge already in the child's possession is still sound, Herbartians made teaching procedures artificial and gave teachers a means of indoctrination by specifying the "steps" to be followed rigidly. By indoctrination is meant a type of undesirable yet effective teaching in which the teacher predetermines the outcome of an inquiry by choosing certain types of materials and/or teaching procedures. For example, we can readily influence the outcome of a study of communism. By following the Herbartian steps we may begin our study by first reminding students of either the evils of wanting something for nothing or the virtues of sharing one's wealth with the needy. If the *preparation* is based on a discussion of the evils of wanting something for nothing, we guide the students to conclude that communism is undesirable and therefore it should be despised. On the other hand, if we begin with a discussion about the virtues of sharing our wealth with the needy, we undoubtedly will encourage our students to regard communism as a desirable and admirable world view. The apperceptive theory of teaching did not, either in principle or in fact, lead to the kind of critical and creative thinking, and the self-inquiry which are so essential in a democratic society where the quality of life depends so much on the enlightened thoughts and conduct of the public. Notwithstanding the Herbartian contribution to the development of scientifically based pedagogy,

> the fundamental theoretical defect of this view lies in ignoring the existence in a living being of active and specific functions which are developed in the redirection and combination which occur as

54. *Ibid.*, p. 71.

they are occupied with their environment. . . . The philosophy is eloquent about the duty of the teacher instructing pupils; it is almost silent regarding his privilege of learning. It emphasizes the influence of intellectual environment upon the mind; it slurs over the fact that the environment involves a personal sharing in common experiences. It exaggerates beyond reason the possibilities of consciously formulated and used methods, and underestimates the role of vital, unconscious, attitudes. It insists upon the old, the past, and passes lightly over the operation of the genuinely novel and unforeseeable.[55]

As was indicated in the beginning of this chapter, Herbartianism remained dominant in American teachers' education as late as the mid-1920s. In recent years it is no longer a moving force in American education, yet we still find a number of current educational practices which are reminiscent of key features in the apperceptive theory of teaching. Here are some examples. Today many experienced teachers firmly believe that effective teaching must be preceded by formulation of a formal lesson plan specifying not only the teaching procedures and steps to be used but also the materials, activities, and sequence by which they are to be presented. The kind of conclusion to be reached in the study is also a part of such a plan. Similarly, prospective teachers are frequently taught how to prepare a systematic instructional sequence and follow it faithfully. They are also told that in presenting new subject matter the teacher must begin with those materials that are most closely related to the learner's immediate interest rather than follow some logical order in which the subject matter is organized by experts in the field. In curriculum development we are still very much concerned with building an educational program in which various disciplines can be interrelated. These practices can, of course, be justified and defended on other, non-Herbartian grounds. Admittedly, it is difficult to determine exactly how many practices are direct consequences of the Herbartian influence.

55. *Ibid.*, pp. 71–72.

But they are often defended on the grounds that it is primarily the teacher's responsibility to select and present instructional materials to the pupil, whose major role is to receive what is offered. Furthermore, when we consider the fact that we still have professors of education who were educated either by Herbartians or by those strongly influenced by Herbartians, it is not unreasonable to argue that in many instances the practices mentioned are remnants of the apperceptive theory.

STRUCTURAL PSYCHOLOGY

What made structuralism so significant in the history of psychology was its firm adherence to experiment and objective observation as methods of studying man's mental states. Thus, as a movement it gave up the traditional metaphysical and speculative interest in the nature of man's soul as a special entity. Psychology became an empirical science in the hands of structuralists. But since direct observation of other men's mental states was not possible, they relied primarily on introspection as the chief method of their scientific investigation. Unfortunately, the introspective reports given by untrained individuals were ambiguous and variable, for different perceptual experiences were often reported with similar verbal expressions, while similar perceptions were frequently described with different terms. In addition, the observer's emotions tended to affect the reports seriously. In order to minimize these ambiguities and the variability of the observers' verbal behavior, structuralists required that psychologists be given rigorous training so that they could analyze their experiences into elementary sensory components which then could be described with a common vocabulary. By using a common vocabulary, variability was to be minimized and clarity achieved. The training and the analysis consisted of the subject's reporting the physical attributes of such sensations as hot, cold, sweet, and salty. In other words, structuralists believed that every human experience could be introspectively reduced to certain irreducible sensations, "raw sensations." It is true, of course, that Wundt and his followers did not originate the introspective method, but they did introduce controlled conditions under which the method could be employed.

No doubt the stringent training given to the psychologists reduced variability in the observational reports, but introspection as the chief method of psychology had a number of serious shortcomings. The first difficulty is that not all experiences are reducible to "raw sensations." For example, how could such complex experiences as hating, loving, trusting, and believing be analyzed into elementary sensations? Even if we could identify those sensations which usually accompany these experiences, combinations of sensations alone do not always add up to hating, loving, trusting, or believing. Consequently, introspective analysis of complex mental states in terms of elementary sensations is likely to be either esoteric or untrue to real experience. Secondly, observers, even with training, may still analyze the same external stimuli into different sensations. For instance, the same food may taste spicy to one person and bland to another. This clearly suggests that the meaning of present experience is influenced by our backgrounds and our contexts as well as our physical conditions. The requirement that complex experiences be analyzed into the same constituent elements is too narrow, rigid, and therefore unsound. Moreover, the background and the language of the observer are an inherent part of the process of observation (i.e., we see things as this or that, or we regard experiences as religious or aesthetic, etc.), hence it is impossible to make introspective reports invariable.

The third difficulty of the introspective method arises when an observer looks at his own emotional state. Here, the observer and the observed are identical, therefore the detached attitude that is necessary for scientific observation becomes impossible to attain. Structuralists readily recognize this difficulty. Consequently, they suggest that we see introspection as *retrospection* in a situation of this sort. That is, the observer should allow himself to go through the emotional experience without interruption, then later he can describe his conscious memory of the experience in an objective manner. But such a procedure is most likely to suffer from memory errors. Yet, from the structuralist point of view, there is no other way of observing such mental (emotional) states. Lastly, if introspection is the only scientifically acceptable and reliable method of observation in psychology, then any study of the conscious processes of small children, the mentally disturbed, and animals is impossible, because these subjects cannot be trained to observe their own conscious states. Here Titchener recommends that we *introspect by analogy.* In other words, the observer first studies the behavior of the subject, e.g., a child, then he attempts to "place himself in the subject's shoes" to see what experience the subject is undergoing. The difficulty here is that the scientific value of such introspection by analogy depends on its verifiability, and therefore, it is necessary that small children, the mentally disturbed, and animals be able to introspect so that their observational data can be compared with the observer's. But of course, if these subjects could observe and report on their own mental processes objectively we would not need to introspect by analogy. In addition, the observer's interpretation of the subject's experience cannot be separated from the observer's own background, knowledge, and bias. Hence, the worth of such data in scientific investigation is open to serious question.

In evaluating structural psychology, we find its scope too limited and its method overly narrow and rigid. But we must not forget that the structuralists' insistence on empirical methodology and its associationistic concerns prepared the ground for a much more empirically rigorous psychology. Indeed, its shortcomings should not distract us from recognizing the contributions made by structuralists in bringing science to psychology.

HUME'S BUNDLE-THEORY

It is logically possible to regard the mind as an unextended substance and also to insist that its functions be studied empirically. Yet the nature of such mind-substance cannot be known scientifically, because an entity without any sensible properties is not amenable to empirical investigation. As Wundt remarked, "'substance' is a metaphysical surplusage for which psychology has no use,"[56] because its existence is not essential in explaining man's mental functions. Here, Hume can be properly credited with providing the needed philosophical basis for both structuralism and later associationistic psychology by repudiating the self as an unextended substance and asserting that the mind is a bundle of sensations which can be examined objectively, systematically, and empirically. From the Humean perspective, it was possible to explain the structure of mental states by formulating empirical generalizations about how impressions and ideas are combined to form man's various conscious states. These generalizations, or laws of association, are publicly verifiable and natural in that they describe the objective relationships (similarity, contiguity, and causality) between certain elementary mental processes. For Hume, associations occur automatically when these relationships are present between ideas and impressions. This implied that there is no separate, inner, spiritual agent, or self, which unifies our elementary experiences. Hence, the mind remained passive.

Hume's rejection of the self as a substance is based on the argument that we never perceive the self, but we are always aware of some particular sensations. This does not necessarily mean that only directly perceived objects exist, for existence of things can be inferred from perceptions. As Bertrand Russell pointed out, no man perceives his own brain but in an important sense he has an idea, i.e., an inferred idea of it.[57] In other words, the fact that we do not perceive the self

56. Wundt, *Lectures on Psychology*, p. 454.
57. Bertrand Russell, *A History of Western Philosophy*, p. 662.

as a simple object does not logically imply that there is no self as an entity, nor does it follow that there is such a self. What does follow is that we cannot know whether there is, and that the self cannot be any part of our knowledge except in an empirical sense. By rejecting the substantial self and making the laws of association solely responsible for the formation of a mind, Hume prepared the ground for more empirical approaches to the mind-body problem. On the other hand, his rejection of the mind as a unifying agent made it difficult for him to give an adequate account of the unity and coherence we "observe" in our experience. For example, let us take the law of similarity. Almost every idea has some similarity with other ideas, but why should certain similarities result in associations but not others? Clearly, if association is to occur between two ideas it is not enough that they are similar objectively, but such a relationship must also be recognizable. A student fails to associate certain ideas with other ideas, not because the ideas themselves lack objective similarity, but because the student is unaware of the relationship. In other words, if Hume wishes to keep similarity as a law of association he cannot retain the mind's passivity. This objection is similar to Immanuel Kant's criticism that the laws of association, viz., resemblance, contiguity, and causality, are not sufficient in explaining how separate sensations are unified into a coherent whole. Kant goes on to point out that association requires memory and memory presupposes an agent that does remembering. He called this agent the *synthetic unity of apperception,* which, as an organizing principle, gives unity to human experience. Whether we agree with Kant or not, his argument does indicate a very serious weakness in Hume's theory of the mind.

To recapitulate Hume's dilemma, while the laws of association do describe how ideas and impressions become connected with each other, they alone cannot give an adequate account of the distinct awareness we have of the unity in our experience. Contrary to Hume's argument, the laws of association presuppose an active mind. The root of Hume's difficulty in accounting for this unity in human experience lies in his artificial world view. Hume sees human experience as an aggregate of discrete and simple sensations connected to each other by the laws of association only. Similarly, he regards the universe as having separate and independent events and objects related to each other only externally in time and space. Yet, even a cursory look at our own process of perception will tell us that we do not in fact begin with discrete and isolated ideas and impressions and then combine them into a coherent whole. On the contrary, we begin with a whole, an experience, and then we break it into separate units for analysis and examination. What we have to remember is that while analysis is necessary, the constituent parts should not be reified or hypostatized. Hume took an experience and analyzed it into a series of simple sensations, which he erroneously assumed to be real and independent entities in themselves. Hume's approach is analogous to a man drawing a straight line and then breaking it up into a number of smaller units, e.g., points. Having done this he concludes that the line is *really* made up of separate and discrete points, which are entities in themselves. He then insists that the continuity we see in the line is only a product of our imagination. If we follow Hume's line of reasoning, an artificial and bifurcated picture of the world is inescapable. Henri Bergson (1859–1941), a French philosopher, raised a similar objection when he wrote:

> On the one hand these concepts [elementary units] laid side by side never actually give us more than an artificial reconstruction of the object [experience], of which they can only symbolize certain general, and, in a way, impersonal aspects; it is therefore useless to believe that with them we can seize a reality of which they present to us the shadow alone.[58]

In this chapter we have examined the apperception or Herbartian theory of teaching in terms of its psychological and philosophical bases. The apperception theory of teaching

58. Henri Bergson, *An Introduction to Metaphysics*, p. 8.

was founded on Herbart's psychology of apperception in its early stages of development, but later it received much of its empirical support from the theoretical insights and experimental findings of structural psychology. Philosophically, structuralism stems from the belief that man's mind consists of certain elementary mental processes, i.e., perceptions. Therefore, understanding of the human mind must begin with an analysis of our mental states into certain irreducible sensations and of the ways in which these constituent units are combined to form various conscious states. In spite of their flaws, the apperception theory, structuralism, and the bundle-theory of mind marked the beginning of a rigorous application of empirical methodology in pedagogy, psychology, and even philosophy. Consequently, metaphysical concepts and "solutions" were repudiated as devoid of any informative meaning.

In the following chapter we shall examine the behavioristic theories of teaching and learning and their impact on the current technology of teaching. We shall also take a critical look at major types of behaviorism, namely, analytic and methodological behaviorism, as well as at some materialistic views of the mind, as a means of scrutinizing the philosophical bases of behavioristic perspectives in education and psychology.

BIBLIOGRAPHY

Bergson, Henri, *An Introduction to Metaphysics*, T. E. Hulme, trans. New York: G. P. Putman's Sons, 1912.

Bode, Boyd Henry, *How We Learn.* Boston: D. C. Heath & Co., 1940.

Dewey, John, *Democracy and Education.* New York: The Macmillan Company, 1961.

Herbart, Johann Friedrich, *The Application of Psychology to the Science of Education*, Beatrice C. Mulliner, trans. New York: Charles Scribner's Sons, 1898.

———— *Outlines of Educational Doctrine*, Alexis F. Lange, trans. New York: The Macmillan Company, 1901.

———— *The Science of Education*, Henry M. and Emmie Felkin, trans. Boston: D. C. Heath & Co.

Hume, David, *A Treatise of Human Nature.* London: J. M. Dent & Sons, Ltd., Vols. I (1956) & II (1940).

McMurry, Charles A., *The Elements of General Method.* New York: The Macmillan Company, 1903.

McMurry, Charles, and Frank M. McMurry, *The Method of the Recitation.* New York: The Macmillan Company, 1926.

Murphy, Gardneer, *Historical Introduction to Modern Psychology.* New York: Harcourt, Brace, & World, Inc., 1949.

Russell, Bertrand, *A History of Western Philosophy*, 3rd ed. New York: Simon and Schuster, 1945.

———— *An Outline of Philosophy.* London: George Allen and Unwin, 1929.

Smith, Norman Kemp, *The Philosophy of David Hume.* London: The Macmillan & Company Ltd., 1964.

Titchener, Edward B., *Textbook of Psychology.* New York: The Macmillan Co., 1919.

Watson, R. I., *The Great Psychologists from Aristotle to Freud.* Philadelphia: J. B. Lippincott Co., 1963.

Wundt, Wilhelm, *Lectures on Human and Animal Psychology*, J. E. Creighton & E. B. Titchener, trans. London: Swan Sonnenschein, & Co., Ltd., 1907.

———— *Outlines of Psychology*, Charles Hubbard Judd, trans. Leipzig: Wilhelm Engelmann, 1907.

Behaviorism and the Technology of Teaching

In this chapter we shall concentrate primarily on Burrhus F. Skinner's (1904–   ) view of teaching and learning, because he, more than any other experimental psychologist, has been explicitly concerned with the systematic application to teaching of recent advances in the experimental analysis of learning. Current interest in programmed instruction, in teaching machines, and in the use of behavioral objectives is the visible effect of Skinner's increasing influence on education. What makes Skinner so significant among, as well as distinct from, the men we have discussed so far is that his main interest lies in the development of a technology rather than a theory of teaching. By the term *technology* is meant "the means of getting a job done, whatever the means and the job happen to be."[1] So in Skinner's case the "technology of teaching" refers to the processes of finding and arranging conditions for learning as well as using physical science and mechanical and electronic devices to make such arrangements more efficient and effective. Thus, teaching is seen as the expediting of learning[2] rather than as an act or an aggregate of acts which actually transmits something to the learner. This suggests that a technology of teaching must be founded on reliable empirical knowledge of human behavior. As we shall soon see, much of Skinner's thought on teaching is directly related to his scientific account of learning. Therefore, in the following pages we shall examine Skinner's view of learning (operant conditioning) together with its implications for teaching. A

1. Robert Dreeben, *The Nature of Teaching*, p. 83.
2. B. F. Skinner, *The Technology of Teaching*, p. 5.

brief study of other behavioristic views will follow this section. The philosophical basis of Skinner's descriptive or radical behaviorism will be discussed in Chapter 5.

OPERANT CONDITIONING

According to Skinner there are two basically different classes of behavior. One is *respondent* behavior, which is elicited by known, specific stimuli. These responses are reflexive and therefore, involuntary. Given the stimulus the response occurs automatically. Bright light and pupillary constriction, a blow on the patellar tendon and the knee jerk, are familiar examples of the connections between stimulus and respondent behavior or reflexes. Some of our reflexes are present at the time of birth, while others are acquired later through conditioning. Conditioning is the process by which an originally inadequate stimulus becomes capable of producing a response after it has been paired with a stimulus adequate in eliciting that specific response. The adequate stimulus and the response to it are called *unconditioned stimulus* and *unconditioned response,* respectively. The inadequate stimuli is known as a *conditioned stimulus,* while a response to it is referred to as a *conditioned response.* For example, Ivan Pavlov (1849–1936), a Russian physiologist, found in a now famous experiment that when food (an unconditioned stimulus) is presented to a dog it leads to salivation (an unconditioned response). He also discovered that by presenting food (an unconditioned stimulus) with a tone (a conditioned stimulus), the latter became capable of causing salivation (a conditioned response) without food being present. Skinner calls this Type S conditioning. In Type S conditioning a specific stimulus is presented to induce a response, and therefore the stimulus always precedes the response. It is to this type of conditioning process that John B. Watson (1878–1958), a leading exponent of early behaviorism, attributed the learning of all responses.

Unlike Watson, Skinner maintained that operant responses account for most of human behavior. Operant responses are emitted by, but not elicited from the organism, and since they are not induced by stimuli they are voluntary in nature. The term *operant* is used to emphasize "the fact that the behavior *operates* upon the environment to generate consequences."[3] In an experiment a rat's lever-pressing response may be made to occur more often by rewarding the rat with food after a correct response. Thus the response is strengthened or *reinforced* by the consequence following it. This then is called *Type R* conditioning in which reinforcement cannot occur unless a response occurs first. Therefore, reinforcement is said to be *contingent* upon responses. The learning of an operant response is called *operant* or *instrumental conditioning* and it differs from Type S or classical conditioning. Skinner points out that

> in operant conditioning we "strengthen" an operant in the sense of making a response more probable or, in actual fact, more frequent. In Pavlovian or "respondent" conditioning we simply increase the magnitude of the response elicited by the conditioned stimulus and shorten the time which elapses between stimulus and response.[4]

It is then the consequence following a response that increases the rate at which an operant response is emitted and the *operant strength* is indicated by this change in the probability of an operant. The following brief account of a Skinner experiment further illustrates the essentials of operant conditioning:

> A hungry rat [is placed in an] experimental space which contains a food dispenser. A horizontal bar at the end of a lever projects from one wall. Depression of the lever operates a switch. When the switch is connected with the food dispenser, any behavior on the part of the rat which depresses the lever is, as we say, "reinforced with food." The apparatus simply makes the ap-

3. B. F. Skinner, *Science and Human Behavior*, p. 65.
4. *Ibid.*

pearance of food *contingent upon* the occurrence of an arbitrary bit of behavior. Under such circumstances the probability that a response to the lever will occur again is increased.[5]

What we have here is Skinner's own formulation or re-formulation of Thorndike's Law of Effect, which asserts that when a response is followed by a satisfying state of affairs the strength of their connection is increased, while the strength of the stimulus-response bond is decreased when the response is followed by an annoying state of affairs.[6] A major difference between Thorndike and Skinner is that the latter is unwilling to use such mentalistic terms as "satisfying" and "annoying" in his explanations, because he holds that a scientific study of human behavior should only describe the observable responses. Therefore, Skinner's version of the Law of Effect simply states that when a response is followed by certain consequences the response tends to appear more frequently. But since not all consequences of a response are reinforcing should we not attempt to find out why some consequences do and others do not strengthen a response? Here Skinner cautions us against speculating about the "whys" of behavior, because

the only way to tell whether or not a given event is reinforcing to a given organism under given conditions is to make a direct test. We observe the frequency of a selected response, then make an event contingent upon it and observe any change in frequency. If there is a change, we classify the event as reinforcing to the organism under the existing conditions.[7]

In other words, a reinforcer is whatever increases the probability of a response. For example, verbal praises, grades, or gold stars given for reading, or even the teacher's smiles which make the learner to behave in a desired way more frequently may be called reinforcers. But we do not know

5. Skinner, *Teaching*, p. 62.
6. Edward L. Thorndike, *Educational Psychology*, Vol. II, *Psychology of Learning*, p. 2.
7. Skinner, *Science and Human Behavior*, pp. 72–73.

why a reinforcer strengthens a response. We only know that some events are reinforcing. Skinner's reluctance to deal with the "why" questions stems from his belief that explanation of an observed fact, i.e., human behavior, should not appeal to "events taking place somewhere else, at some other level of observation, described in different terms, if at all, in different dimensions."[8] Therefore, our knowledge about learning should be based solely on a descriptive study of the variables under which learning occurs without relying on the mental or the physiological processes, because neither of them is accessible to direct observation. It is this kind of empirical knowledge which will enable us to actually shape behavior "as a sculptor shapes a lump of clay."[9] And by arranging appropriate contingencies of reinforcement, or the sequence in which responses are followed by reinforcing events, we can maintain the shaped behavior for a long period of time. Similarly, a complex behavior can be shaped by following a carefully designed program of gradually changing contingencies of reinforcement, which will form small units of behavior thereby successively approximating the desired response.

Now that we have examined the role of reinforcement in operant conditioning generally, we are ready to take a more detailed look at the ways in which various types of reinforcements and punishment affect the teaching-learning process.

REINFORCEMENT

Positive and Negative Reinforcements

As was pointed out earlier, Skinner found no useful answers to the question "Why is a reinforcer reinforcing?" But we do know that some things are reinforcing when they are present in a situation, while others strengthen an operant

---

8. B. F. Skinner, "Are Theories of Learning Necessary?" *The Psychological Review*, Vol. 57, No. 4, July 1950, p. 193.
9. Skinner, *Science and Human Behavior*, p. 91.

response when they are withdrawn. A *positive reinforcer* is, then, a stimulus which, when added to a situation, increases the probability of a response, while a *negative reinforcer* is any event, which when withdrawn, produces the same effect. For instance, an increased appearance of the rat's lever-pressing response as a result of presentation of food following the response is a case of positive reinforcement. Withdrawal of electric shocks which results in the increased performance of a pigeon's pecking activity illustrates *negative reinforcement.* What we must remember about these reinforcers is that, whether positive or negative, they are both defined in terms of their effect, i.e., strengthening of a response. Hence, we must not confuse negative reinforcement with punishment, which is a basically different process from reinforcement. What is commonly called punishment involves either withdrawal of a positive stimulus, e.g., food, or presentation of a negative stimulus, e.g., an electric shock.

Conditioned Reinforcement

When a stimulus, let us say a plate, which originally does not have any reinforcing power is paired with a reinforcing (primary) stimulus such as food, the former frequently acquires the same reinforcing property as the primary stimulus. This process is called *conditioned reinforcement* and the plate, in this case, is called a *conditioned reinforcer.*[10] Conditioned reinforcers are often the result of natural contingencies, i.e., food is usually presented on a plate. Now, when conditioned reinforcers are paired with more than one primary reinforcer the conditioned reinforcers are said to be generalized.[11] Money is a good example of a generalized reinforcer, for it enables us to secure food, clothing, shelter, and entertainment. Students behave or study for grades, scholarships, or diplomas, which are not as readily exchanged with other

10. Skinner, *Science and Human Behavior,* p. 76.
11. *Ibid.*, p. 77.

primary reinforcers as is money. But they are indeed exchangeable with high-paying jobs and prestige. The practice of tokenism as seen in our schools today is an excellent example of the use of generalized reinforcers. The term *tokenism* refers to the practice of giving tokens to children for certain acts and/or achievements and allowing them to cash in the tokens for extra recess periods or other activities of their choice. Attention, affection, approval, and permissiveness are examples of other kinds of generalized reinforcers. The teacher's attention is reinforcing, because it is a necessary condition for other reinforcements from him. And the child cannot receive any reinforcement from his teacher unless he can attract the teacher's attention. This suggests that anything that attracts the attention of teachers and parents, who are likely to supply other rewards, will be reinforced. Of course, attention alone is not enough, because the teacher tends to reinforce only those acts which he approves. Consequently, the responses, such as submissiveness, which lead to such signs of approval as a smile or verbal praise will be strengthened.

Generalization of reinforcement is particularly important in teaching because *stimulus induction* or transfer of learning takes place through this process. Transfer of learning is said to have occurred when "the reinforcement of a response increases the probability of all responses containing the same elements."[12] As an illustration, if we reinforce a pigeon's response of pecking a yellow round spot one square inch in area, the effect of this reinforcement will spread so that the pigeon will peck a red spot of the same size and shape because of the common properties of size and shape. The pigeon will also respond to a yellow square spot of one square inch in area because of its color and size and to a yellow round spot two square inches in area because of the similar elements of color and shape. What all this means is that in order for transfer of learning to occur the learner must be able to

12. *Ibid.*, p. 94.

perceive similarities between the original and the new stimulus situations. Though Skinner might not agree with this statement—because an organism's perception of similarity is not an observable event—instances of inappropriate behavior due to misperception of similarities in certain situations are abundant.

Schedules of Reinforcement

Much of human behavior is shaped through operant conditioning. But the ways in which operant responses are shaped in everyday life are slow and inefficient, mainly because reinforcements of these responses do not occur in either a regular or a uniform manner. Thus if we are to be effective and efficient in shaping and maintaining desired responses, we must construct schedules of reinforcement. Such schedules are especially important in forming a complex behavior, which must be shaped gradually through selective reinforcement of certain responses but not others.

The schedule in which reinforcement follows every response is called *continuous reinforcement.* This schedule is generally used in getting an organism to emit the desired response. But very rarely are we reinforced continuously. We do not win every time we play a game of chess nor do we catch fish every time we go fishing. "The reinforcements characteristic of industry and education are almost always intermittent because it is not feasible to control behavior by reinforcing every response."[13] Hence, in *intermittent reinforcement* only some of the responses are followed by reinforcing events. If reinforcement is regular, say at two- or five-minute intervals, it is called *interval reinforcement.* In this schedule the rate of responding is determined by the frequency of reinforcement. If we reinforce a response every two minutes, the response occurs more frequently than if reinforcements are presented every five minutes. Another

13. *Ibid.,* p. 94.

kind of intermittent schedule is *ratio reinforcement* in which the frequency of reinforcement depends on the rate at which operant responses are emitted. So, if we decide to reinforce every third response it is called reinforcement at a fixed ratio. Students receiving grades upon completion of a paper, a salesman selling on commission, and a workman's piecework pay are all examples of fixed ratio reinforcement. Of course, interval and ratio schedules can be combined so that responses can be strengthened according to the passage of time as well as the number of unreinforced responses emitted. Skinner reports that there are sufficient experimental data to suggest that generally the organism gives back a certain number of responses for each response reinforced, implying that there is a direct relationship between the frequency of response and the frequency of reinforcement. But now what happens to responses if they are not reinforced?

The effect of a nonreinforcing situation is called *operant extinction.* In other words, if a response is not followed by any reinforcement for a period, the response becomes less and less frequent until eventually it completely ceases. Thus, unrewarded acts of children often cease to occur, and though operant extinction takes place much more slowly than operant conditioning, it is an effective means of removing an unwanted behavior from the organism's repertoire. However, extinction should not be confused with forgetting, because "in forgetting, the effect of conditioning is lost simply as time passes, whereas extinction requires that the response be emitted without reinforcement."[14]

DRIVES AND EMOTIONS

In explaining a man's behavior we often attribute his actions to certain drives he is supposed to have. We might say

---

14. *Ibid.*, p. 71.

that John ate a lot of food to satisfy his hunger drive or that he drank a quart of lemonade to quench his thirst. But Skinner does not regard drives as stimuli which causally effect the rate at which responses are emitted. Only in a metaphorical sense do drives cause our actions. As Ernest R. Hilgard, a contemporary American learning theorist, reiterates, "the word drive is used [by Skinner] only to acknowledge certain classes of operations which affect behavior in ways other than the ways by which reinforcement affects it."[15] Hence, *drive* is simply a convenient way of referring to the effects of depriva tion and satiation. Deprivation or the hunger drive can be defined operationally by withholding food from an organism, say a rat, to the point where the rat reaches about 80 percent of its normal body weight, while satiation can be demonstrated by feeding the rat until it no longer takes any food. In terms of their effects, deprivation usually strengthens a response but satiation decreases the rate of a response. These operations can be applied to practical situations, for instance by prohibiting a child from having snacks so he will eat well at the regular meal time, or by serving large portions of salad and bread before the main course so that a rather skimpy dinner can be served without complaint. Skinner believes that drives should not be treated as special inner states causing overt responses. Similarly, emotions are not inner causes of behavior. As Skinner insists, the terms *anger, love,* and *hate* are different ways of talking about a person's predispositions to act in certain ways, because

> the names of the so-called emotions serve to classify behavior with respect to various circumstances which affect its probability. The safest practice is to hold to the adjectival form. Just as the hungry organism can be accounted for without too much difficulty . . ., so by describing behavior as fearful, affectionate, timid, and so on, we are not led to look for *things* called emotions. The common idioms, "in love," "in fear," and "in anger" suggest

15. Ernest R. Hilgard, *Theories of Learning,* p. 97.

a definition of an emotion as a conceptual state, in which a special response is a function of circumstances in the history of the individual.[16]

In consonance with Skinner's account of drives and emotions, motivation, too, should not be thought of as an inner force propelling an organism to action. It is merely an expression which conveniently covers deprivation and satiation.

OPERANT CONDITIONING AND THE TECHNOLOGY OF TEACHING

Teaching and the Problem of the First Instance

As Skinner himself has put it so explicitly, the application of the principles of operant conditioning to teaching is simple and direct, for teaching is a matter of arranging contingencies of reinforcement under which students learn. They do, of course, learn without being taught, but by providing appropriate learning conditions we can speed up the occurrence of behavior which would have either appeared very slowly or not appeared at all. In this sense, the teacher does not actually pass along some of his own behavior; he builds or helps to construct the behavior of the student, who is induced to engage in forms of behavior appropriate to certain occasions. And since operant conditioning is the process by which man learns all of his voluntary behavior, the technology of teaching becomes a matter of providing and arranging the necessary conditions with the help of mechanical devices, electronic instruments, and schedules of reinforcement so that desired learning can occur efficiently and effectively. Teachers must then help their students to reach an appropriate instructional objective by progressive approximation. This means using reinforcement to form small units of desired terminal behavior. In operant conditioning, reinforcement cannot be presented unless the responses have actually occurred. In other

16. Skinner, *Science and Human Behavior*, pp. 162–163.

words, we must wait until a desired response appears so that it can be strengthened. But in education many and complex terminal behaviors must be established within a limited period of time. Therefore, it would be tedious and inefficient for teachers to wait for desired responses to appear. In fact, some responses may never take place without some form of deliberate inducement. How to bring about the wanted behavior without simply waiting for it thus becomes "the problem of the first instance."

Skinner indicates a number of possible solutions to the problem of the first instance. One is to force a behavior physically, as we often squeeze a child's hand around a pencil and move it to form letters. Unfortunately, the child is not writing in any real sense and if he does learn to write there are probably other variables at work. Another possibility is to evoke a response by some stimulus. For example, a teacher may raise his hand or wave an object conspicuously to induce his students to pay attention to his story telling. This technique, too, has a weakness in that the elicited attention is not the attention the students eventually learn. Consequently, these two measures are useful only in a small range of teaching-learning situations. A more effective technique is to prime certain desired responses. Primed behavior can be induced through such procedures as movement duplication, product duplication, and non duplicative repertoires.

Movement Duplication   Skinner seems to be convinced that man has an innate tendency to behave as he has observed others behave. When a person acts as others do, he is naturally reinforced. Hence, the teacher can utilize his students' tendency toward imitative behavior by reinforcing those responses which resemble the responses of a model, often the teacher himself. Since "movement duplicating contingencies are most effectively acquired when the model is conspicuous,"[17] the teacher as a model can repeat the desired responses slowly and even with exaggeration. A student's

17. Skinner, *The Technology of Teaching*, p. 208.

imitative response can be made conspicuous by recording his speech or letting him watch himself in a mirror or by video taping the responses. Examples of movement duplication can be found in drama, physical education, and dancing courses where students are made to "copy" the teacher's gestures and movements.

Product Duplication   Movements cannot be imitated readily if the model's actions cannot be seen. Of course the effects of a model's movements can be duplicated and therefore the movements of the learner and the model need not be similar. We can learn to pronounce certain words, deliver a line in a play, or paint a picture by imitating a model, the teacher, without actually seeing how the model himself has performed these acts. What is important here is that the outcome, that is the product, be similar to that of the model's, but not the movements. Learning to speak a foreign language with records or copying a singer's style by listening to a recording are examples of product duplication. Again, product duplicating contingencies are made more effective if the model and the product are as clear as possible. For instance, a foreign language student may be allowed to listen to his own pronunciation through earphones and a tape recorder. The modern language laboratory is an excellent example of mechanical devices helping to improve product duplicating contingencies.

Nonduplicative Repertoires   In Skinner's own words, "behavior may also be primed with the help of pre-established repertoires in which neither the responses nor their products resemble controlling stimuli."[18] To put it simply, we can tell the student what to do or how to act and then reinforce him when he acts according to our instruction. What we are doing is giving a verbal instruction to evoke a certain response with the help of behavior patterns which have already been established. Though the evoked response is different from the established responses, through the latter's help we can give

18. *Ibid.*, p. 210.

the student a "picture" of what he must do. This technique is certainly more efficient and convenient than shaping behavior by progressive approximation or by product or movement duplication.

Of course, the techniques of priming behavior do not replace other means of shaping behavior. But they do help us with the initial stages of establishing desired behavior and hence they are useful tools in the early phase of teaching. Skinner reminds us that we should not mistake simple execution of behavior as learning. Teachers often become satisfied merely if their students repeat after them because the student's imitative behavior is often reinforcing for the teacher. Skinner warns us that

> students [can] make the same mistake when they study. They take notes during a lecture or when reading a book, they recognize, transcribe, and outline them, they underline words to serve as primes and then read them with special intensity. In so doing they respond to priming stimuli and emit behavior of the proper form. But they are not necessarily bringing that behavior under the control of new variables.[19]

In short, learning takes place because behavior is reinforced, but not merely because it has been primed. Learning can be said to have occurred only if the learner can make similar responses on his own.

The reinforcers used in most formal learning situations to establish desired behaviors are artificial in the sense that they are deliberately contrived. Therefore, in school, grades and praise are used to reinforce those responses which make up our teaching objectives. Such artificial reinforcers are necessary because natural reinforcers take too long a time to be effective. For example, no student learns to think critically because he can immediately win in a debating contest, nor do children learn to plant seeds because they are promptly reinforced by the resulting harvest. In fact,

19. *Ibid.*, p. 212.

the human race has been exposed to the real world for hundreds of thousands of years; only slowly has it acquired a repertoire [of responses] which is effective in dealing with that world. Every step in the slow advance must have been the result of fortunate contingencies, accidentally programmed. Education is designed to make such accidents unnecessary. . . . The natural contingencies used in education must almost always be rigged.[20]

Any teacher who relies solely on natural contingencies of reinforcement has given up his role as a teacher, for to expose the student to his environment gives no guarantee that the student's behavior will be followed by any reinforcing event. Therefore, contrived reinforcers are essential in learning and the work of arranging an effective sequence of such reinforcers should take up much teaching activity.

Programmed Instruction and Teaching Machines

If by using priming techniques we have been successful in getting our students to execute certain behavior, we have begun the process of shaping terminal behavior, i.e., teaching objectives. We must then arrange a great many contingencies of reinforcement in order that the students can perform the same act on their own and maintain it. Clearly, teaching in the context of schooling involves much extremely complex terminal behaviors. Even at the elementary school level most instructional objectives go far beyond such relatively simple tasks as making letters or coloring pictures. As we go up the educational ladder, objectives become more involved and subtler. Behaviors of such great complexity cannot be learned all at once, but must be formed through programmed instruction. Programmed instruction is a process of successively approximating teaching objectives by making an efficient use of reinforcers to establish, maintain, and strengthen desired responses. As Skinner cautions us, in programming it is important that the learner "understand" each step before he

20. *Ibid.*, p. 155.

moves on to the next. This means the learner stays in one stage until he masters what he has to learn to move on to the next stage. At least in principle, however, programmed instruction is more than a matter of shaping terminal behaviors simply by dividing it into smaller units and reinforcing them one by one. A subject, or a skill such as critical thinking, is more than a mere aggregate of individual responses, for the smaller units are related to each other in such a way that they, as a whole, possess varying degrees of coherence and consistency. Moreover, in programmed instruction each new unit of learned behavior should add to already established behaviors in a cumulative way so that terminal behaviors can be reached successively. Consequently, it is not enough that the smaller units are of proper size; they must also follow an effective sequence. For example, very rarely can we arrange the various parts of a subject in a line, because they usually form a network or a "tree." In other words, the student has to cover many different segments of a subject matter at the same time. Hence, "the steps in a segment must be arranged in order, and segments must be arranged so that the student is properly prepared for each when he reaches it."[21] Putting a subject in sequence can be done according to the complexity of the materials, or the difficulty of the terminal behavior, or the logical structure of the subject, or a natural order inherent in the subject (e.g., history can be taught as a chronological sequence of events). Unfortunately, none of these approaches to sequence has proven itself consistently useful. As Skinner points out, the most advantageous and effective programming is accomplished when sequence is based on the teacher's knowledge of the student's attainment and direction. Consequently, "arranging effective sequences is [a] good part of the art of teaching."[22]

As Skinner reports in his *Cumulative Record,* he has recorded many millions of responses from a single organism

21. *Ibid.,* p. 221.
22. *Ibid.,* p. 223.

during thousands of experimental hours.[23] In *Schedule of Reinforcement,* published in 1957, Skinner summarized about 70,000 hours of the continuously recorded behavior of individual pigeons, consisting of approximately one quarter of a billion responses. These data were presented in 921 separate charts and tables with almost no interpretive or summarizing comments. The sheer number of responses which make up behavior makes clear that any personal attempt at an effective arrangement of contingencies without some sort of mechanical device is unthinkable. If the control of animal behavior requires an elaborate mechanical arrangement, the contingencies of reinforcement for shaping and maintaining human behavior would certainly necessitate mechanical help, because man is much more sensitive to precise contingencies than lower organisms. The so-called teaching machines are, then, such instruments. They can help the teacher to apply the latest advances in the experimental analysis of learning from teaching. Skinner's description of the machine concisely explains the ways in which it functions:

> The device consists of a box about the size of a small record player. On the top surface is a glazed window through which a question or problem printed on a paper tape may be seen. The child answers the question by moving one or more sliders upon which the digits through 9 are printed. The answer appears in square holes punched in the paper upon which the question is printed. When the answer has been set, the child turns a knob. The operation is as simple as adjusting a television set. If the answer is right, the knob turns freely and can be made to ring a bell or provide some other conditioned reinforcement. If the answer is wrong, the knob will not turn. A counter may be added to tally wrong answers. The knob must then be reversed slightly and a second attempt at a right answer made. (Unlike the flash-card, the device reports a wrong answer without giving the right answer.) When the answer is right, a further turn of the knob engages a clutch which moves the next problem into place in window. This movement cannot be completed, however, until the sliders have been returned to zero.[24]

23. B. F. Skinner, *Cumulative Record,* p. 154.
24. *Ibid.*

There are many different versions of the machine with various features to make its operation more automatic and sophisticated, but the basic function they perform in facilitating learning conditions is essentially the same.

One of the advantages in utilizing teaching machines as an instructional aid is that right responses can be immediately reinforced. Often manipulation of the machine will be reinforcing enough to keep the child at work. Also, a single teacher can supervise an entire class working with such machines and at the same time help each child to move at his own rate. In this way gifted as well as slow children can learn without being deterred by the fact that one teacher cannot individually supervise children of such diverse capacities and needs. Furthermore, the machine makes it possible to present subject matter so that the solution of one problem depends on the answer to the preceding problem. The student can eventually progress to a complex repertoire of behaviors. There are still other benefits from teaching machines. Like a good tutor the machine carries on a continuous interchange with the learner and induces constant activity to keep the learner alert. The machine also "demands" that a given point be completely understood before moving on to the next because it presents only those materials for which the student is ready. Like a skillful tutor the machine helps the student to come up with the right answer and it shapes, maintains, and strengthens correct responses by reinforcing them promptly. Moreover, it is possible to present through the machines programs when appropriate courses or teachers are not available. And individuals who cannot be in school for various reasons can "teach" themselves with the machine.

If teaching machines can indeed function as effectively as teachers, will they eventually replace teachers? As Skinner rightly points out, teaching machines do not teach in any literal sense at all. They are labor-saving devices and, therefore, only the mechanized aspects of teaching have been given to machines. This arrangement leaves more time to teachers to carry on those relationships with pupils which cannot be duplicated by an instrument. Teaching machines enable teachers to work with more children than they could ever hope to without instrumental aid. Of course, the use of these machines will change some time-honored practices. For example, traditional grades or classes will cease to be significant indicators of the child's academic growth; since the machine's instruction makes sure that every step is mastered, grades or marks will be important only as a means of indicating how far a child has advanced. Most of all, A, B, C, D, and F will no longer serve as motivators in the traditional sense, and the fact that each child is permitted to work at his own rate may lessen if not eliminate the social stigma which usually comes with being a slow learner or an underachiever.

It is indeed possible that teaching machines and the techniques of programming can be misused to produce submissive individuals who lack both initiative and creativity. On the other hand, the technology of teaching can help us to maximize the development of human potential of those attributes which can make the greatest possible contribution to mankind. Skinner correctly insists that the harm or the benefit coming from the use of teaching machines and programmed learning is not inherent in the technology of teaching. Man must decide what goals are worthiest of pursuing both for the individual and his society. The technology of teaching is only one means of achieving an educational end, and machines and programs should not dictate the direction of our education.

PUNISHMENT

The use of punishment as a means of controlling human behavior is as old as man. In school we use various punishments to influence children's behavior. Poor academic work is punished with failing grades, while recess periods are often taken away to make children less noisy. Unfortunately, punishment as a technique of controlling human behavior does not always work effectively. Children do not become quiet for any significant length of time by having their recess periods taken away, nor does imprisonment seem to decrease criminal behavior. Certainly, failing grades do not cause children to do better academic work. If what has been said about punishment is true, what role does it play as a variable in shaping and maintaining behavior?

In the process of learning, "reinforcement builds up [responses]; [but] punishment is designed to tear them down."[25] Punishment weakens a response in the sense that it decreases the rate of an operant, but it does not permanently reduce the organism's tendency to respond. That is, "the effect of punishment is a temporary suppression of the behavior, not a reduction in the total number of responses."[26] According to Skinner, even after the severest and most prolonged punishment the rate of response rose when punishment was discontinued. In other words, the occurrence of the punished behavior is simply postponed rather than permanently eliminated. Moreover, since suppression of unwanted behavior does not either specify or reinforce desirable behavior, punishment is an ineffective means of correcting a child's misbehavior. In punishing a child all we are doing is arranging conditions under which acceptable behavior could be strengthened without clarifying what behaviors are acceptable. As was pointed out earlier, nonreinforcement is a much more effective means of removing unwanted responses permanently.

Punishment leads to unfortunate by-products, especially for teachers, because it often becomes the source of conditioned stimuli evoking incompatible behavior from students. That is, anything that becomes associated with the punished act can turn into a conditioned stimulus. Frequently, unwanted emotional reactions such as fear and anxiety result from punishment. Therefore, if a child is punished for eating noodles with his fingers he may stop eating noodles or cease to eat at all. If certain sexual activities before marriage are

---

25. Skinner, *Science and Human Behavior*, p. 182.

punished, such acts, though socially approved after marriage, may become associated with such emotional predispositions as guilt, shame, or even a sense of sin. These emotional by-products make it extremely difficult for teachers to establish a productive relationship with their pupils. Understandably, Skinner suggests that we avoid using punishment and find other means of weakening undesirable responses. Briefly, unwanted behavior can be weakened or controlled by modifying the circumstances. Certain behavior of young children may be allowed to pass according to developmental schedule and the children allowed to "grow out" of their behavior naturally. Often conditioned responses can be weakened and eliminated by simply letting time pass. Of course, the most effective means of weakening responses is extinction. For example, a child who throws objects to attract the teacher's attention may be allowed to continue his deed without the reinforcement of attention. Another technique is to strengthen incompatible behavior through positive reinforcement. If a child attempts to gain his teacher's attention by leaving his seat and disturbing others, the teacher may pay attention to the child only when he remains in his seat, thereby strengthening the desirable behavior which is incompatible with his early undesirable behavior. In short, direct positive reinforcement is preferable to punishment, because this approach seems to have fewer of the objectionable by-products usually associated with punishment.

In general, punishment is a poor means of controlling pupil behavior. While punishments often temporarily postpone unwanted behavior, students can and do act to avoid aversive stimulation, i.e., punishment. They may find many different ways of escaping; they may daydream or become inattentive or stay away from school altogether. Another unfortunate result of punishment is that the students may counterattack; they may attack openly or they may simply become rude, defiant, and impertinent. Today physical attacks against the teacher are not an impossibility. If the severity of punishment is increased, counterattacks become more frequent and one party withdraws or dominates the scene. Vandalism and unresponsiveness are other consequences of punishment. Usually the reactions to punishment are accompanied by such emotional responses as fear, anxiety, anger, and resentment so that establishment of an educationally productive teacher-pupil relationship becomes almost impossible. Therefore, Skinner recommends that teachers minimize or eliminate the use of punishment as a means of controlling pupil behavior. One way of accomplishing this is to eliminate the conditions which give rise to punishable behavior. For instance, we can separate children who cannot get along with each other, furniture can be made rugged enough so that children cannot damage it, and other means of lighting can be substituted for windows thereby doing away with the possibility of children breaking them or becoming distracted by the activities they see outside. In other words, we should provide conditions in which punishable behavior is not likely to occur and at the same time we should construct programs in which children will be able to succeed most of the time. Another possibility is to reinforce those behaviors which are incompatible with the unwanted behavior. As Skinner puts it, "students are kept busy in unobjectionable ways because 'the devil always has something for idle hands to do.' The unwanted behavior is not necessarily strong, but nothing else is at the moment stronger."[27] So, if a student persistently disrupts the class he might be asked to lead a class discussion or he could be given the responsibility of managing certain segments of the class's activities, and so on.

According to Skinner's evaluation, education today is too dominated by aversive stimuli. Children work to avoid or escape from a series of minor punishments, which may come in the form of the teacher's criticism or ridicule, being sent to the principal, suspension, or even "paddling." "In this welter of aversive consequences, getting the right answer is in itself an insignificant event, any effect of which is lost amid the

27. *Ibid.*, p. 190.

anxieties, the boredom, and the aggressions which are the inevitable by-products of aversive control."[28] In addition to this predominantly punitive atmosphere, the contingencies of reinforcement are far too few and whatever contingencies we have arranged are loose and unsystematic. That is, our schools not only lack carefully planned schedules of reinforcement but too much time lapses between reinforcements given to children. Not infrequently days and even weeks pass before assignments and tests are returned to students with grades. We are also without carefully planned programs to help children advance through a series of progressive approximations to the terminal behavior desired. For Skinner, children's failure and incompetence are direct results of these shortcomings which reflect the inefficiency and the ineffectiveness of our schools. Such a sorry state is in part attributable to the teachers' failure to understand and apply the recent advances in the experimental analysis of learning.

OTHER BEHAVIORISTS ON LEARNING

There is no doubt that Skinner's theory of learning has left an indelible mark on today's technology of teaching, but the views of other behaviorists are not without important implications. Edwin Guthrie's work deserves some attention, for he represents a molecular approach to the study of human behavior which is much more extreme than Skinner's descriptive behaviorism. The interpretations Clark Hull, O. Hobart Mowrer, and Edward Tolman give to the role of drives, emotions, and purpose should be of a special interest to us, because the Skinnerean system assigns relatively little significance to these variables which most teachers regard as central in the teaching-learning processes. Therefore, in the following several pages we shall discuss very briefly the views of Guthrie, Hull, Mowrer, and Tolman.

28. Skinner, *Cumulative Record*, p. 150.

Guthrie on Contiguous Learning

Skinner's analysis of learning is said to be molecular in the sense that he is interested in specific and observable responses which make up larger behavioral patterns or molar behavior such as problem solving, critical thinking, and so on. Edwin R. Guthrie (1886–1959), another behaviorist psychologist, preferred molecular analysis of human behavior. However, for him behavior consists of irreducible movements, a complex combination of which make up what Skinner calls a response. Hence to Guthrie an act or a response is an abstract way of talking about an aggregate of movements and nothing more. Accordingly, learning is seen as an all-or-nothing affair in which stimulus and response become connected to each other at their first pairing, or in one trial. The learning process is then explained in terms of the contiguity of stimulus and response. In Guthrie's own words, "a combination of stimuli which has accompanied a movement will on its recurrence tend to be followed by that movement."[29] In other words, if a stimulus is followed by a response (a movement) once, that response is likely to occur again. And as long as the stimulus is paired with the response, learning will continue to take place. As some readers may have noted already, Guthrie does not subscribe to Skinner's "law" of operant conditioning or to Thorndike's Law of Effect, which emphasizes reinforcement as an important condition for learning. This means that according to Guthrie's theory the most vital variable in learning is the *contiguity* of stimulus and response.

When a number of stimulus-response patterns take place, e.g., putting together a puzzle or struggling through a new piece of music on the piano, it is the last response in the series that is learned. This is what Guthrie calls the principle of *postremity.* The principle asserts that the learning of new responses keeps on occurring as long as the organism continues to respond to existing stimulus situations or until such

---

29. Edwin R. Guthrie, *The Psychology of Learning*, p. 23.

time as there are no more stimuli. Now, if Guthrie is right, then the practice of responses is not necessary, because a response is learned at the first instance of its pairing with a stimulus. But do we not in fact benefit from practice? Guthrie explains that the same stimuli are not likely to recur in exactly the same way, therefore it is necessary to learn individual responses in relation to a great many variations of stimulus patterns. Thus what is commonly thought of as practice is a matter of learning many separate movements in response to many stimuli. It is this kind of learning that enables us to act appropriately in various situations that are said to be similar. Guthrie further reminds us that learning an act such as bicycling requires the learning of an extremely large number of movements and that many responses are errors, which are of no value to the learner. Hence, what is often taken to be practice is the pairing of stimulus and response until appropriate responses are made.

In Guthrie's system the learning of a response is attributed to stimulus-response contiguity (connection) rather than reinforcement. Yet rewards and punishments are believed to affect the learning process in an indirect way. A response that was learned at the first instance of its pairing with a stimulus remains until another event occurs to break up the already established connection. Reward or reinforcement then functions in such a way as to prevent the breaking up of the learned connection. In short, reinforcement is an effective means of stopping the organism from forgetting what it has previously learned; for Guthrie forgetting occurs because new learning replaces what has been learned, but not because of disuse or a lapse of time. As for the extinction of behavior, since Guthrie does not subscribe to the Law of Effect, extinction has no significant meaning in contiguous conditioning. However, the role of punishment in learning is determined by what it causes the organism to do. That is, if punishment changes the unwanted behavior it is because it elicits an incompatible behavior. If punishment does not work, it is because an incompatible behavior is not evoked.

For example, we may slap the wrist of a child who constantly reaches out for other children's belongings. If the slapping punishment is severe enough it will elicit the withdrawing response which is incompatible with the reaching-out response.

Some Implications for Teaching Since all learning takes place as a result of the contiguous connection of stimuli and movements, teaching should not be merely a matter of telling children to be critical, careful, or self-reliant. Teaching must be specific instead of general and whatever is going to be taught should be divided into its smallest units. Thus, in teaching a unit of a subject all the important questions should be specified and the required answers be precisely indicated. And as the principle of postremity suggests, children ought not to be allowed to leave a learning situation with incorrect responses. The teacher must make sure that the last response which occurs is a correct one. From Guthrie's perspective it is essential that the learner be led to an appropriate learning objective and since learning and unlearning depend on the ways in which the teacher presents certain stimulus-response patterns, the teacher must always be in charge of teaching-learning situations.

Hull on Learning as Drive Reduction

Unlike Skinner, behaviorist Clark L. Hull (1884–1952) was interested in building a general theory of learning based on a number of postulates from which theorems and their corollaries could be logically deduced. Hence, Hull's system is not based on scientifically established laws, but it is founded on certain basic assumptions which are to be checked and tested by empirical generalizations. Disagreeing with Skinner, Hull contended that scientific theory or explanation is more than a collection of observation statements about a particular state of affairs. He states: "in science an event is said to be explained when the proposition expressing it has been logically derived from a set of definitions and postulates coupled with certain observed conditions antecedent to the event."[30] Accordingly, Hull's theory of learning is built on eighteen postulates.[31] However, we shall limit our discussion to only a few of the assumptions which have direct bearing on teaching.

Primary Reinforcement Like Skinner and Thorndike but unlike Guthrie, Hull holds that learning occurs as a result of reinforcing a particular stimulus-response or receptor-effector connection. He makes no distinction between operant and respondent behaviors as Skinner did. He asserts that responses take place only as reactions to stimuli and therefore, the organism must be aware of the stimulus in order to react to it. Thus, while Hull subscribes to the Law of Effect his formulation of it differs from that of Skinner. For Hull,

> whenever an effector activity occurs in temporal contiguity with the afferent impulse, or the preservative trace of such an impulse, resulting from the impact of a stimulus energy upon a receptor, and this conjunction is closely associated in time with the diminution in the receptor discharge characteristic of a need, there will result an increment to the tendency for that stimulus on subsequent occasions to evoke that reaction.[32]

To put it simply, whenever a response following a particular stimulus situation results in a reduction of a drive, a reinforcement, the particular stimulus-response pattern is strengthened and the response is likely to recur in similar situations. To illustrate this principle, if an athlete's act of chewing gum reduces his nervousness (a drive), he is likely to chew gum again when he finds himself in a similar stressful situation. A careful study will show that there are at least three important assumptions underlying Hull's version of the Law of Effect. They are: (1) no learning can occur unless there is a drive which can be reduced by a response and therefore, motivation is essential to learning; (2) learning occurs as a result of

30. Clark L. Hull, *Principles of Behavior*, p. 3.
31. In the 1943 edition of his book, *Principles of Behavior*, Hull listed only sixteen postulates. But his later work, *Essentials of Behavior*, published in 1951 contained eighteen postulates.
32. Hull, *Principles of Behavior*, p. 80.

drive-reduction but the drive need not be completely eliminated; (3) learning takes place cumulatively so the learner must
go through steps of varying size. Hull thinks that there was
experimental evidence to suggest that the greatest amount of
learning takes place during the early period of practice and the
least amount of learning occurs in the final stage. This implies
that learning not only occurs continuously and in increments
but also without being directly observed.

Secondary Reinforcement Any stimulus which becomes
associated with a primary response and reduces a drive
acquires the same reinforcing power as the primary response.
And any stimulus which is connected with primary drive, e.g.,
fear, takes on the same properties belonging to the primary
drive. Hull calls this *secondary drive.* For example, if a neutral
stimulus, say the sound of a siren, is followed by the painful
stimulus of a tornado the neutral stimulus is likely to bring
about fear, which was originally evoked by the actual effects
of the tornado. In short, the principle of secondary reinforcement accounts for much of the human learning related to
intellectual and social behavior. While Skinner is unwilling to
say why some events are reinforcing, Hull maintains that any
event which reduces a drive has reinforcing power.

Reactive Inhibition Another postulate with important
ramifications for teaching is *reactive inhibition.* According to
this postulate every response tends to cause some negative
aftereffect. It "produces in the organism a certain increment
of fatigue-like substance or condition which constitutes a
need for rest."[33] If rest is not given, this fatigue-like condition
inhibits response, and if an organism is made to carry out a
response continuously without rest it will eventually cease to
respond. Only rest can restore the organism's reactive capacity.

*The Goal Gradient Hypothesis and the Fractional-
Antedating Response* The goal gradient hypothesis states
that learning occurs more effectively as the organism ap-

---

33. *Ibid.*, p. 391.

proaches its goal. The closer the organism gets to the goal the more active it becomes; the responses which are closest to reinforcement are learned more readily. Therefore, in learning a sequence of activities the last of the sequence is learned first, while the first of the sequence is learned last. The concept of the fractional-antedating goal response refers to the anticipatory quality of certain learned behavior. In other words, the organism can perform a certain portion or a fraction of a goal response such as eating cheese at the end of a maze before it actually reaches the desired end. A rat salivates before it reaches its goal, the chunk of cheese at the end of a maze. Hence, the rat's salivating response is anticipatory in nature or has an antedating quality. The act of spreading a napkin on your lap and taking a drink of water at a restaurant have this antedating quality in that by being fractions of the terminal response they anticipate a goal response of eating a meal.

Some Implications for Teaching   Though Hull deliberately refrained from becoming concerned with practical applications of his learning theory, his theory still has significant ramifications for teaching. It should be clear by now that in Hull's system the presentation of stimuli is most vital in both animal and human learning. This means that the teacher has the responsibility of becoming a source for various stimuli which will activate the learner's reactive power. The teacher ought to select and arrange instructional materials and techniques in such a way that the learner will feel the need to solve the problems stemming from his surroundings.

In learning a series of activities it is important that each step is learned and reinforced until all parts of the final objective are learned equally well, because the response that is closest in time to the goal is learned most effectively. According to Hull learning occurs gradually and in increments. Therefore, the teacher should not be too discouraged by the fact that children often do not learn quickly. He must also remember that there is a limit to the activities a learner can perform; excessive drills and exercises hinder rather than promote effective learning.

Tolman on Purposive Behavior and Learning

In his analysis of human behavior Skinner completely rejected variables which were not directly observable. Consequently, he dismissed such mentalistic terms as *purpose, insight, drive,* and *expectancy* as explanatory fictions. Guthrie is still more atomistic in his approach because he is primarily interested in individual movements rather than whole acts as the "raw" materials of human behavior. As might be expected, he too shies away from terms referring to mental states as causes for overt responses. In Hull's work we found such terms as *goal,* and *drive,* but his account of learning remained overwhelmingly physiological. Unlike these other men, psychologist Edward C. Tolman (1886–1951) was seriously concerned with constructing a theory of behavior which could account for cognitive and purposive behavior as well as for overt responses. He inquired into the ways in which purposes, expectancies, and drives influence human behavior and became convinced that these mentalistic terms could be translated into behavioristic terms with objective behavior as their referent. Therefore, Tolman's system is at once behavioristic and purposive. The expression "purposive behaviorism" appropriately describes both his philosophical perspective and scientific methodology. However, Tolman himself prefers to call his psychology "operational behaviorism" to emphasize his method of defining the concepts in such a manner that "they can be stated and tested in terms of concrete repeatable operations by independent observers."[34]

Purposiveness of Behavior   According to Tolman the basic characteristic of molar as opposed to molecular behavior is that it is goal directed, or purposive. Hence, in all human behavior, except the reflexes, "a certain *persistence until* character is to be found."[35] This means that most of man's voluntary responses are not mere reactions to stimulus situations but attempts to reach a goal. Consequently, Tolman

---

34. Edward Chace Tolman, *Behavior and Psychological Man,* p. 115.
35. *Ibid.,* p. 33.

insists that the more significant explanations of behavior are descriptions of organisms moving toward or moving away from something. *Purpose* is then defined in terms of "going toward" or "going away" motions,[36] and the process of learning, too, can be explained in terms of such motions. The fact that organisms use "paths" and "tools" in reaching a goal makes molar behavior not only purposive but also *cognitive* in nature.

Intervening Variables Tolman found that the stimulus-response theory was not able to explain adequately complex aspects of human behavior. He was convinced that there were other factors between stimulus and response which influenced behavior. Cognition, purpose, appetite, bias, and demand are several examples of such intervening variables. Further, Tolman thought that eventually we would be able to measure the degree of influence which any given intervening variable would have on a response. What makes the concept of intervening variables so important is that it takes into account the personal nature of behavior, which gives different meanings to similar responses emitted by different individuals. For example, two men digging ditches assign different meanings to their work. It is important, then, to know the reasons for an act if we are to understand its meaning accurately.

Sign Learning According to Tolman's theory, learning is a process of arranging and rearranging intervening variables (means-ends objects) to achieve a goal. In this process it is more important to learn the meanings of signs than movements. In other words, learning involves following a sort of map, i.e., a cognitive map, so an objective can be reached. The learner also acquires "expectancies," because when a new stimulus *(sign)* is followed by a second stimulus *(significate)* which has an already established meaning, the learner will associate them. For example, if a child has always purchased popsicles from a white jeep with a colorful canopy and a

36. *Ibid.*, pp. 35–36.

jingling bell, he will expect the jeep and/or the popsicles whenever he hears the sound of the bell. The most essential aspect of learning is that the sign-significate sequence is presented frequently. Reinforcements or rewards are important only because they emphasize the direction of behavior; they do not directly lead to learning. Punishments, though they deter certain behavior, regulate learning in a way similar to reinforcement. In Tolman's system practice was significant only to the extent that it helped build up *sign Gestalts,* which are learned relationships between environmental variables and the organism's expectations that certain things will lead to certain other things. A pattern of sign Gestalts that an organism has built up at any given time is called a *cognitive map* and learning often results in a change in this map.

Latent Learning In a number of experiments Tolman found that learning takes place without any reward or reinforcement. Rats were allowed to explore a maze without any food at its terminal point. Later when food was placed at the end of the maze these rats were able to find the shortest route to the food as efficiently as those rats who went through similar trials with the reward (food) present throughout. Data from experiments of this type convinced Tolman that learning takes place as a result of exploration and observation and without any reinforcement. In other words, the rats learned sign Gestalt or pattern in the maze, which remained latent until such time as the reward of food motivated the rats to execute appropriate actions to reach their goal. The reward regulated behavior only by emphasizing its direction.

Some Implications for Teaching Though Tolman's interest leans more toward the study of animal learning, his theory of purposive behaviorism with cognition playing the leading role has some significant ramifications for teachers, who are primarily concerned with learning as it relates to the attainment of certain purposes and goals. For instance, the concept of sign Gestalt is particularly important in teaching, because effective and desirable teaching in school should involve the learner's understanding of the ways in which various factors of his psychological world relate to the achievement of his goal. Learning is more than the acquisition of a repertoire of specific acts or movements. Both inside and outside the school, learning should have a cumulative effect so that the child can become increasingly capable of handling the various indeterminate situations in which he finds himself. In this type of learning there are likely to be frequent changes in the child's cognitive map. Also he learns not because he is given immediate reward but because he sees the meanings of his environmental variables and their relationship to future goals. Furthermore, since sign Gestalts of one situation can cover other circumstances, children should be encouraged to evaluate situations and problems not in terms of apparent and superficial characteristics but in terms of sign Gestalts. Such encouragement will increase the transfer of what was learned in one subject to others.

The notion of sign learning suggests that learning can take place as a result of being shown or told. Neither "doing" nor rewards are imperative. And if we take Tolman's account of latent learning seriously, then we must not take observable actions as the only indicators of learning. Obstacles and barriers still need to be removed, however, and appropriate motivating conditions be provided so that the child can perform what he has learned.

Mowrer on the Two-Factor Theory of Learning

O. Hobart Mowrer's (1907–   ) work in the study of human behavior is largely concerned with the process by which emotional reactions—which have received little attention from other behaviorists—are learned. Like Hull, Mowrer holds that reinforcement does lead to drive reduction, but unlike Hull and Guthrie he distinguishes between voluntary reflexive responses and voluntary responses. Initially, Mowrer maintained that classical conditioning and operant conditioning could adequately account for the learning of these two different types of responses. Consequently, in the early formulation of his theory involuntary reflexive responses were said to be learned through classical conditioning, in which any stimulus that becomes paired with an unconditioned stimulus (like pain eliciting fear) acquires the power to bring about the same response. This was called *sign learning.* On the other hand, *solution learning* or learning of voluntary responses was explained as the result of operant or instrumental conditioning. For example, fear is first learned through sign learning; the learned fear then acts as a drive to activate the organism to a response, which is reinforced if and when it reduces the drive, i.e., the fear. In other words, an organism learns to avoid or to escape from those conditions which produce fear reactions. Let us say that a child was stung by a bee and experienced pain. The sight of the bee then becomes a conditioned stimulus eliciting fear, an emotional response. The child has now learned the fear of bees through sign learning. Later when the child sees another bee his fear response is elicited. If he runs away and avoids the bee his act will reduce fear. Thus the voluntary response of running away is reinforced by reduction of a drive.

In recent years Mowrer has revised his earlier theory by maintaining that both sign learning and solution learning share certain characteristics so that "all learning thus reduces . . . to sign learning and all extinction to a reversal of the meanings of signs."[37] Returning to the boy and the bee sting example, the sight of a bee became a conditioned stimulus for fear and the child's own sensation of perceiving the bee became a sign of danger. Similarly, the sensation from the child's act of running away also became a sign of relief or hope. In other words, by running away the child feels safer, because the sensation from the running response reduces his fear drive. Therefore, both types of learning can be reduced to sign

37. O. Hobart Mowrer, *Learning Theory and Behavior*, p. 427.

learning. An important implication of Mowrer's theory is that learning occurs in connection with pain as much as with pleasure.

Some Implications for Teaching   If Mowrer is correct that learning is a matter of conditioning emotional responses rather than of acquiring acts and muscular movements, then a child does not need to *do* something in order to learn it. Learning could take place merely by listening or watching. This implies that showing and telling (lecturing) can be effective means of teaching. It also implies that punishment can be used to control the learner's behavior. Since punishment produces fear which inhibits certain unwanted responses, it results in withdrawal or avoidance responses. Punishment in Mowrer's view works effectively only if it produces fear, therefore it should not be defined as any specific measure such as taking away recess periods or standing in the corner of a room, for they do not necessarily lead to fear responses. This is probably the reason a punitive measure does not affect all children.

CONCLUDING COMMENTS

As Skinner pointed out several times, the most important task of the teacher is to arrange the conditions under which desired learning can occur. Considering the fact that the teacher is expected to bring about changes in extremely complex behavior, he should be a specialist in human behavior. Effective and efficient manipulation of the multitude of variables affecting children's intellectual as well as social behavior cannot be accomplished by trial and error alone, nor should such work be based solely on the personal experiences of the teacher, which cover only a limited range of circumstances. Consequently, a scientific study of human behavior is vital in the improvement of teaching, because it provides us with the accurate and reliable knowledge about learning from which new instructional materials, methods, and techniques can be derived. Similarly, an empirical analysis of the teaching process is essential, for it clarifies the teacher's responsibility by specifying the terminal behaviors which can be achieved through a series of small steps and progressive approximations. This approach makes teaching practices more specific, thereby facilitating a more effective evaluation. More importantly, the introduction of technology to teaching enables the teacher to act as a human being. That is, programmed instruction and teaching machines free the teacher from routine chores and also from the need to maintain the learner's behavior by aversive control. The teacher can relate to his students not merely as a taskmaster but as a guide and an adviser who is concerned about their present interests and future goals. Furthermore, technology makes it possible for the teacher to teach more than he knows because it allows him to "arrange all the necessary contingencies, even when he himself has never been exposed to them."[38] To sum up the value of technology in teaching Skinner remarks that

> in the long run a technology of teaching helps most by increasing the teacher's productivity. It simply permits him to teach more—more of a given subject, in more subjects, and more students. . . . We cannot improve education simply by increasing its support, changing its policies, or reorganizing its administrative structure. We must improve teaching itself. Nothing short of an effective technology will solve that problem.[39]

One of the more evident results of the behaviorist influence in education is the recent emphasis on the use of behavioral objectives as a means of defining educational and instructional aims. By "forcing" teachers to specify the kind of observable behaviors which are to result from their teaching efforts, they are made to be much more precise about the materials and methods to be used in their work. On a larger scale, the behaviorist psychology of learning has played a major role in the development of ten comprehensive elementary teacher

---

38. Skinner, *The Technology of Teaching*, p. 257.
39. *Ibid.*, p. 258.

education models funded by the United States Office of Education and developed by a group of major universities. Although these models have individual differences in presentation and program content, all of them are "behavioral" in their approach to teacher education. In these models we see an application of such behaviorist concepts as schedule of reinforcement and successive approximation to the development of a technology of teaching. Each model is divided into a number of major areas of study, which are in turn divided into sub-areas. The instructional objectives of these areas are then stated in behavioral terms and series of program modules, or instructional units, are planned to achieve these objectives by progressive approximation. For example, the Michigan State University model has six major areas of study constituting the entire elementary teacher education program. They are: (1) Clinical Experience, (2) General-liberal Education, (3) Scholarly Modes of Knowledge, (4) Professional Use of Knowledge, (5) Human Learning, and (6) Continued Professional Development.[40] The modules are computer-coded and each student can complete them at his own rate. In the Michigan State model there are 3,000 or more modules. The sections on "Scholarly Mode of Knowledge" and "Professional Use of Knowledge" alone contain approximately 1,200 and 600 modules respectively. In order to complete an elementary teacher education program of this type a prospective teacher must study individual modules, which are the smallest instructional units. The nature and function of the following module taken from "Scholarly Modes of Knowledge" are almost self-explanatory:[41]

We can, of course, view our educational and instructional goals as involving a number of specific actions, but this does not mean that these objectives are mere aggregates of separate and observable acts. To use a trite phrase, the whole *is*

40. Michigan State University, *Behavioral Science Elementary Teacher Education Program,* Final Report, Project No. 8-9025, Volumes I, II, & III.
41. *Ibid.,* p. VI–39, Vol. II.

*OBJECTIVES	GIVEN HYPOTHETICAL DIAGNOSIS OF MIDDLE SCHOOL PUPIL'S WORD	00485017
	RECOGNITION SKILLS. LEARNER WRITES APPROPRIATE	00485018
	INSTRUCTIONAL PLAN.	00485019
*PREREQUISITE	SUCCESSFUL COMPLETION OF PREVIOUS MODULES, PARTICULARLY	00485020
	481	00485021
*EXPERIENCE	CANDIDATES FOR MIDDLE SCHOOL TEACHING LISTEN TO AND	00485012
	DISCUSS WITH INSTRUCTOR PARTICULAR TECHNIQUES FOR TEACHING	00485013
	WORD RECOGNITION SKILLS IN MIDDLE SCHOOL. EMPHASIS IS ON	00485014
	TECHNIQUES FOR TEACHING STRUCTURAL ANALYSIS, DICTIONARY,	00485015
	ETC.	00485016
*SETTING	SMALL GROUP (1-12 STUDENTS), COLLEGE	00485011
*MATERIALS	RESULTS OF HYPOTHETICAL DIAGNOSIS OF WORD RECOGNITION	00485005
	SKILLS OF MIDDLE GRADE PUPILS.	00485006
*LEVEL	GRADES 5-8	00485009
*GENERAL	GENERALIST	00485008
*HOURS	1/4	00485007
*EVALUATION	LEARNER CORRECTLY WRITES APPROPRIATE INSTRUCTIONAL PLAN	00485022
	FOR DEVELOPING WORD RECOGNITION SKILLS OF 3 HYPOTHETICAL	00485023
	MIDDLE SCHOOL PUPILS.	00485024
*FILE	WORD RECOGNITION INSTRUCTIONAL TECHNIQUES MIDDLE SCHOOL	00485010

greater than the sum of its parts. For example, critical thinking requires (1) knowledge of the rules of formal logic, (2) the ability to apply the rules, (3) the detection of hidden assumptions, and (4) identification of fallacious uses of language. Yet, thinking critically means more than executing these individual acts separately, for when we say that a child can think critically we usually mean he can deal with a problematic situation by relating it to past events, the present context, and also future possibilities. Hence, this kind of thinking requires the use of the total of the individual's experience and of his knowledge of the ways in which it is related to an indeterminate situation. Let me illustrate further. In an elementary science program prepared for the early grades by the American Association for the Advancement of Science the steps necessary in teaching scientific thinking were listed as (1) observing, (2) using space/time relationships, (3) using numbers, (4) measuring, (5) classifying, (6) communicating, (7) predicting, (8) inferring. But "observing" is not separable from "using space/time relationships" or "using numbers." In a real sense "observing" involves all of these steps with the possible exception of (7), yet it would be incorrect to maintain that scientific thinking is nothing more than observing, using space/time relationships, using numbers, and so on. We can, of course, work with a child so that he becomes skillful in using space/time relationships and numbers, in measuring, in classifying and in communicating. But we must go beyond exercises and drills in specific skills and show the child how the supposedly separate elements of scientific thinking are inextricably related to each other, and to perspectives, and to the cognitive map, as it were. Therefore, it is essential that children be allowed to deal with complex situations by taking into account the intellectual, the social, and even the emotional contexts from which various problems arise and are perceived. Preoccupation with specific acts alone will likely make the child become inflexible, mechanical, and routine oriented in his life style.

Another area of education in which descriptive behaviorism has made significant contributions is the development of programmed instruction and of teaching machines. Notwithstanding Skinner's claim that programmed instruction will enable teachers to teach more things to more students in a more efficient and effective way, numerous objections have been raised against these developments in education. One of the more frequent complaints is that the use of teaching machines and programmed materials is tantamount to treating children like animals, because the procedures and devices used in programmed instruction were originally employed in studying animal behavior. The critics go on to insist that what works for rats and pigeons will not necessarily work for man. However, Skinner retorts by saying that "what is common to pigeons and man is a world in which certain contingencies of reinforcement prevail."[42] Hence, regardless of how the devices and programs were developed, if they do produce desired consequences there should be no objections against them just because they are also used in working with animals.

Programmed instruction is also criticized for its use of contrived (artificial) contingencies of reinforcement. It is argued that in real life we do not do everything for reinforcements (rewards) and when we receive rewards they are

42. Skinner, *The Technology of Teaching*, p. 84.

usually natural consequences. But Skinner points out that the teacher who waits for natural contingencies (reinforcements) will be ineffective, for his responsibility is to arrange necessary contingencies so that a behavior can be learned and later become useful. For example, a mother reinforces her child in learning to talk so that the child's verbal behavior will become useful in the future. At first, the child's efforts are reinforced with such contrived reinforcers as kisses, praises, and cookies. Only later is the child's verbal behavior naturally reinforced. Even adults do not learn responses because they are naturally reinforced. As a matter of fact, much of what is learned in school is due to contrived, not natural, contingencies; students study for grades, honors, diplomas, and so on.

Programmed instruction is condemned by some as a means of regimentation, which is inconsistent with democratic education. While programmed instruction can be used to produce submissive individuals, it is not inherently regimenting. Here Skinner agrees that technology can be used unwisely to produce docile people, but he also observes that it can be utilized to "maximize the genetic endowment of each student; it could make him as skillful, competent, and informed as possible; it could build the greatest diversity of interests; it could lead him to make the greatest possible contribution to the survival and development of his culture."[43] This is a slightly exaggerated estimate of what technology can accomplish, but Skinner rightly insists that the regimenting or liberating consequences of programmed instruction are not as dependent upon the concept of programming as upon what values we hold to be worthwhile ends of education. In other words, regimentation does not necessarily follow from the use of programmed instruction. It is, finally, our own decision of how a technology of teaching ought to be used that determines its consequences.

To the cry that teaching machines will replace teachers,

43. *Ibid.*, p. 91.

Skinner replies that mechanical devices will free a teacher from his routines and allow him to devote more of his time to advising and counseling students. In a sense any teacher who does not see his responsibility as broader than the mechanical functionings of a teaching machine deserves to be replaced by it. Education is as much an intellectual affair as a moral and cultural process, and therefore its aims must go beyond developing skills and imparting information. This means that education must go on in a social, moral, and intellectual climate in which children can learn to maintain all sorts of relationships with others and become increasingly capable of dealing with various problematic situations. Hence, programmed instruction and teaching machines should be regarded as helpful teaching aids and nothing more.

A frequently mentioned benefit of programmed instruction is that it can provide individualized instruction for children with varying capacities and rates of achievement. Indeed, the use of programmed materials and teaching machines can help a child learn at his own rate without hindering others of greater or lesser abilities and levels of attainment. But this is only one aspect of individualized instruction. That is, individualized teaching should make it possible for each child not only to complete the learning materials at his own rate but also to pursue and develop his own interests and perspectives. Since what is learned through the programmed approach is predetermined, instruction becomes individualized only in the sense of permitting a child to work at his own rate. Moreover, this kind of teaching interferes with the spontaneous and creative aspects of certain learning processes, because it is not possible to prepare programmed materials that can individually accommodate the unique interests of all the children in a single classroom, let alone an entire school. Because programmed materials usually provide a limited number of answers to the questions posed, the child may be restricted in the variety of perspectives from which he can examine an issue. In addition, since working with teaching machines usually requires mechanically choosing one right answer from several possible answers already provided, the child is given little opportunity to develop the skills of written and oral communication particularly in an aesthetic and creative sense.

Consequently, the behavioral approach to education as found in the ten models mentioned earlier may lead to an efficient and effective, but narrow and rigid, technology of teaching. Skinner's suggestion that we improve the teacher's effectiveness in arranging appropriate contingencies of reinforcement and thereby lessen, if not eliminate, the predominantly punitive climate of the traditional classroom, is quite sound. But we should remember that machines are not the only means of facilitating conditions for learning nor is it true that all children in our schools learn only to escape from aversive stimuli. Learning as related to schooling is an extremely complex process which is affected by many variables. Among these are such factors as the socio-cultural milieu of the society, the teacher's own personality, the child's background and interests, and even the physical and the fiscal state of the school. Therefore, no single variable should be regarded as solely responsible for the amount of learning taking place as a result of teaching. One of the potential dangers of the concept of accountability, which has attracted much attention from school administrators, parents, and teachers, is that in our urgent desire to improve teaching effectiveness we may hastily adopt such a simple criterion as the scores on standardized achievement tests as the sole means of measuring teaching effectiveness, thereby assuming that the teacher is the only variable directly responsible for the occurrence of learning. First we need to determine the factors which the teacher can directly control and manipulate to affect the child's learning process; then we may hold the teacher accountable for the extent to which he has been successful in providing such an influence.

There can be no argument against the view that improvement of teaching must be based at least in part on sound scientific knowledge of learning, nor can there be serious disagreements about the potentiality of programmed instruction and teaching machines in freeing the teacher from his routine chores and hence enabling him to devote his efforts to more important aspects of teaching. Particularly in view of rapid scientific and technological progress and the resulting changes in human needs and conditions, it behooves us to look for ways in which the scientific knowledge of human behavior and a technology of modifying it can help us become increasingly efficient and effective in our work as teachers and educators. But though we grant that these things are beyond dispute, we can still legitimately raise questions about the adequacy of Skinner's psychology and its pedagogical implications.

As we have seen, Skinner explains the learning of all voluntary actions in terms of operant conditioning. In other words, our voluntary responses occur because they are reinforced. Even verbal behavior such as giving a lecture on behaviorism and the technology of teaching is thought of as behavior reinforced through the mediation of others who, as listeners, respond to the speaker in such a way as to strengthen his behavior.[44] And because of his atheoretical bias, Skinner is unwilling to deal with the question "Why do reinforcers reinforce?" other than to say that they do in fact increase the probability of a response. There is little doubt that in an analysis of animal behavior or simple human responses this reinforcement view is adequate. Moreover, if it were the case that all of our educational and instructional objectives dealt with relatively simple responses, Skinner's operant conditioning might be sufficient. But to a great extent our instructional objectives have to do with complex skills, attitudes, and beliefs which cannot be expressed completely in terms of directly observable responses. Questions about the child's purpose and intention almost always and necessarily arise in dealing with teaching-learning situations. Not only do our purposes and intentions affect our conduct but the interpretation others give to them influences their conduct, which in turn changes our attitudes and behavior. For exam-

44. B. F. Skinner, *Verbal Behavior*, pp. 2, 224–226.

ple, if you are hit by a baseball, your reaction to the incident depends upon how you understand the intentions of the person who threw the ball. If you decide that the ball accidentally hit you, you might walk away, but if you conclude that the ball was deliberately thrown at you, you might take a considerably different course of action. I am not, of course, suggesting that there is a world of intentions which is distinct from the world of physical events. But I am suggesting that Skinner's reinforcement language cannot adequately deal with the kinds of phenomena which are usually called mental.

For Skinner the term motivation refers to deprivation, which can be operationally defined. This means whatever we say about the motives behind a man's decision to join the Peace Corps, study the philosophy of science, or deliver a lecture on behaviorism, they must be regarded as deprivation of some sort. But what kinds of deprivation? Deprivation of affection, attention, success, recognition, and so on are not acceptable to Skinner as explanatory terms because they are not observable behavior. It would certainly be strange to say that Skinner wrote the book *Verbal Behavior* because he had been deprived of something. Similarly, only in a trivial sense can we say that the utterances of a philosopher or of Skinner himself are nothing more than reinforced responses. In fact, if we take Skinner's account of verbal behavior seriously we must conclude that his own statements regarding the validity of behaviorism are nothing more than emitted verbal responses reinforced through the mediation of other persons. In other words, Skinner says that behaviorism is valid because the act of saying is reinforced by others. Whatever he says about descriptive behaviorism amounts to no more than emitted responses reinforced by others. But this hardly demonstrates the validity of his or any other point of view, for the properties which make a judgement valid are something other than reinforcement from others. The statement "Behaviorism is valid" no more makes behaviorism valid than the statement "Behaviorism is false" makes it false. If behaviorism is valid there must be at least one exception to its basic principle that all voluntary human behaviors are nothing more than reinforced responses. The assertion "Behaviorism is valid" must be based on something more than reinforcement from other persons. Skinner would no doubt persist in saying, "Behaviorism is valid" even if his audience, or even perhaps the entire world population disagreed with him, precisely because his saying so was not brought about by concurrence (reinforcement) from others. In a paper delivered at the meeting of the American Psychological Association in September, 1968, Skinner admitted that at present experimental analysis could not give an adequate account of complex verbal behavior. He also indicated that in the future behaviorism will give us an adequate explanation of such complex behavior. But can descriptive behaviorism do what Skinner promises? I think not, because Skinner's brand of behaviorism is based on a very narrow and rigid positivistic philosophy of science. (We shall take a closer look at this issue in the following chapter.)

Finally, we need to examine Skinner's reinforcement theory, because it is so central to his psychology that any weakness in it will raise serious doubts about the validity and adequacy of his account of learning and teaching. Quite consistent with Skinner's antitheoretical perspective, his reinforcement theory is based on direct observation of the functional relationship between operant responses (dependent variables) and their causes (independent variables). Hence, it is not an inferred but a descriptive theory. However, as an empirical explanation its validity depends upon its verifiability. In other words, are there instances which confirm the claim that a response does occur more frequently when followed by reinforcement? Furthermore can this proposition be shown to be false if appropriate evidences can be found? Though the second of the two questions may appear strange to some readers, it is as important as the first because

all tests can be interpreted as attempts to weed out false theories—to find the weak points of a theory in order to reject it if it is falsified by the test. . . . Because it is our aim to establish theories as well as we can, we must test them as severly as we can; that is we must try to falsify them. Only if we cannot falsify them in spite of our best efforts can we say that they stood up to severe tests. This is the reason why the discovery of instances which confirm a theory means very little if we have not tried, and failed, to discover refutations.[45]

In other words, to validate an empirical theory we must not only look for the kinds of events which support the theory but we must also know and search for the sorts of evidence which, if found, would refute the theory. A theory is said to be valid if we find a sufficient number of confirming instances without also discovering events that could falsify it. For example, consider the statement "The sound of a buzzer which consistently follows the flashing of a bright light causing a child to blink his eyes will later induce the same response in the child without being paired with the flashing of a bright light." This would be true if (1) we find supporting evidences and (2) if we do not discover instances in which the buzzer did not produce the blinking response.

Now, returning to Skinner's view of reinforcement, we can indeed find numerous cases which would confirm the assertion that an operant response increases in its probability when followed by a reinforcing situation. Children's increased interest in reading resulting from receiving gold stars or tokens of some sort from their teacher is only one of many such instances. But what sorts of evidences would refute the reinforcement theory? That is, could there be some situations in which a response followed by a reinforcer would not occur more frequently? The answer here is an emphatic No, because a reinforcer is explained in terms of its effect. Since a reinforcer is seen as whatever increases the probability of a response, there cannot be reinforcement without an increase in the occurence of an operant. In short, Skinner's reinforcement theory is not falsifiable. When a supposedly empirical

45. Karl Popper, *The Poverty of Historicism*, pp. 133–134.

explanation turns out to be an irrefutable theory its validity and adequacy become suspect, for no empirical knowledge can go beyond its probable and tentative nature.

For the sake of further clarification let us say that an educational psychologist claims that a child who is given a proper instruction in spelling will never make any spelling errors. The expression "proper instruction," is explained, of course, as whatever enables the child to spell correctly at all times. Now, we should have no difficulty finding children who always spell correctly and have received some instruction in spelling. The fact that they make no spelling errors makes whatever instruction they received the "proper" sort. But could we falsify the educational psychologist's claim by discovering children who, in spite of a proper instruction in spelling, continue to misspell? Of course not, because "proper instruction" is defined in terms of its effect. Hence, if children continue to misspell, we *must* conclude that the instruction they received was not of a "proper" kind. And since the properties of the so-called "proper instruction" which promote correct spelling have not been specified, the assertion cannot be falsified and, therefore, it cannot be thoroughly tested. Because of this irrefutable nature of Skinner's reinforcement theory we must suspect its validity as an adequate explanation of human behavior and the teaching-learning processes. I am convinced that it is this irrefutability which makes Skinner and his followers act as if the reinforcement theory is a certain truth. This attitude seems to be reflected in the Skinnereans' reluctance to consider the possibility that other perspectives in psychology may have substantive contributions to make in understanding human behavior.

In the following chapter we will examine the philosophical basis of descriptive behaviorism by critically analzying its approach to the mind-body problem and the philosophy of science. We shall also briefly consider the neural-identity theory of mind and some possible educational implications of a physicalistic approach to the study of human learning.

BIBLIOGRAPHY

Books

Dreeben, Robert, *The Nature of Teaching.* Glenview: Scott, Foresman and Co., 1970.

Guthrie, Edwin R., *The Psychology of Learning.* New York: Harper Publishing Co., 1952, Revised Edition.

Hilgard, Earnest R., *Theories of Learning.* New York: Appleton-Century-Crofts, Inc., 1956, Second Edition.

Hull, Clark L., *Principles of Behavior.* New York: Appleton-Century-Crofts, Inc., 1943.

Mowrer, O. Hobart, *Learning Theory and Behavior.* New York: John Wiley Sons, Inc., 1960.

Popper, Karl, *The Poverty of Historicism.* London: Routledge and Kegan Paul, 1957.

Skinner, B. F., *Cumulative Record.* New York: Appleton-Century-Crofts, Inc., 1959.

────── *Science and Human Behavior.* New York: Free Press, 1953.

────── *The Technology of Teaching.* New York: Appleton-Century-Crofts, Inc., 1968.

────── *Verbal Behavior.* New York: Appleton-Century-Crofts, Inc., 1957.

Thorndike, Edward L., *Educational Psychology,* Vol. II, *Psychology of Learning.* New York: The Teachers' College, Columbia University, 1913.

Tolman, Edward Chace, *Behavior and Psychological Man.* Berkeley and Los Angeles: The University of California Press, 1961.

Others

Michigan State University, *Behavioral Science Elementary Teacher Education Program,* Final Report, Project No., 8-9025, Vols. I, II, & III. Washington, D. C.: United States Government Publishing Office, October, 1961.

Skinner, B. F., "Are Theories of Learning Necessary?" *The Psychological Review,* Vol. 57, No. 4, July, 1950.

Methodological Behaviorism, Analytic Behaviorism, and the Identity Theory of Mind

As we have seen in the preceding chapter, Skinner regards the learning of all voluntary responses as a process of conditioning in which the probability of a response is increased by reinforcement. This concept of learning is based solely on a description of the ways in which certain variables, responses and reinforcers, are related to each other. Accordingly, *mental faculties, consciousness, apperceptive masses,* and such other mentalistic terms as *motives, insight, understanding, aspiration, intention, love, hate,* and *anger,* are thought of as having only metaphorical meanings at best. Yet, most of us will find it difficult, if not impossible, to deny that we have vivid experiences of understanding, planning, aspiring, loving, hating, and being angry. Further, we often explain the actions of others as well as our own by referring to various mental and emotional states. For example, we might say that John spanked his child because he was angry or that he brought home a gift because he was in a generous mood. But, if it is true that most men do have clear and distinct experiences of undergoing mental and emotional states, why does Skinner choose to ignore them by dealing with the immediately observable responses only? On what grounds does he assert that our inner states, mental or physical, are irrelevant in explaining human behavior? These are important questions, because, to a large extent the answers to them give us the basis for assessing the validity and the adequacy of Skinner's views on the technology of teaching, the learning process, and human behavior in general. In considering these queries we need to examine Skinner's conception of the nature and function of science, for his thoughts on the subject matter and methods of psychology are an integral part of his philosophy of science. Therefore, in this chapter we shall be primarily concerned with a critical study of Skinner's methodological behaviorism as a philosophy of science distinguished from analytic or logical behaviorism. We shall also take a brief look at the identity theory of mind and some possible implications of neurological findings for education.

PSYCHOLOGY: A SCIENCE OF BEHAVIOR

Etymologically, *psychology* is the study *(logos)* of mind or soul *(psyche);* historically, psychology has been concerned with the analysis of mental powers and various forms of conscious states as a means of understanding the nature of the mind, believed to be the cause of all of man's overt actions. Moreover, since the term *mind* stood for an unobserved and unobservable entity inextricably connected to theological and metaphysical issues, it was not amenable to scientific investigation as we understand the expression today. Skinner states:

> If psychology is a science of mental life—of the mind, of conscious experience—then it must develop and defend a special methodology, which it has not yet done successfully. If it is, on the other hand, a science of the behavior of organisms, human or otherwise, then it is part of biology, a natural science for which tested and highly successful methods are available.[1]

Consequently, neither the term *mind* nor *self* has any defensible place in a science of behavior for, according to Skinner, these invented notions together with their special characteristics provide false explanations. Furthermore, since the mind or psychic events are said to lack physical dimensions we have additional grounds for rejecting them. Skinner goes on to

1. B. F. Skinner, "Behaviorism at Fifty," *Behaviorism and Phenomenology,* T. W. Wann, ed., p. 79.

argue that a science of behavior can gain nothing by using mentalistic terms. Hence, to speak of a man's mind is not to speak of some immaterial entity or self but to refer to a "device for representing a *functionally unified system of responses*."[2] This means that psychology as a science of the human mind must become an empirical and experimental science devoted to studying the functional relationship between responses, dependent variables, and their causes, independent variables.

Functional Analysis

The expression *functional analysis* refers to the investigation of the cause-effect relationship between dependent variables and independent variables, which will enable us to predict and control the behavior of organisms. However, the term *cause* as used by Skinner does not imply any mysterious power of a variable to produce another event, for "a cause is simply a change in the independent variable and an effect is a change in the dependent variable."[3] Therefore, when Skinner asserts that "A caused B" he means that A is followed by B or that B is preceded by A. Like Hume, Skinner does not assume any metaphysical glue supposed to connect a cause with its effect, because he regards the cause-effect relationship as a conjunction between two events, cause and effect. This makes it possible to say "If A, then always (or probably) B" rather than "A makes B happen." Through a functional analysis of human behavior we gain information about its causal relationships and by synthesizing these facts in quantitative terms we can come to have a "comprehensive picture of the organism as a behaving system."[4] But such analysis requires that we confine ourselves to the description rather than the explanation of responses. In addition, the concepts

2. B. F Skinner, *Science and Human Behavior*, p. 285.
3. *Ibid.*, p. 23.
4. *Ibid.*, p. 35.

used to describe the responses must be defined in terms of immediate observations without assigning to them either mental or physiological properties.[5] In other words, any concept which does not have an observable referent should not be used in a scientific explanation of man's behavior.

Inner States

It would appear that many of man's overt actions are caused by certain neurophysiological and/or mental processes. If this is true, would we not do better to study the relationship between these inner states and overt responses? To this Skinner firmly replies that knowledge of inner states is of little value to a science of behavior because inner states are not directly observable. Because they are not observable it is easy to assign properties to them without justification and to invent spurious explanations.

Neurophysiological States Skinner opposes the use of neural or physiological conditions as explanations of human behavior not only because direct observation of the nervous system (or physiological change) has never been made but also because these conditions can only be inferred from overt behavior. Even if these physical processes could be directly observed, "they could not justifiably be used to explain the very behavior upon which they were based."[6] In any case, we do not yet have neurophysiological knowledge based on direct observation about the conditions which precede an instance of verbal behavior (saying "No, thank you,") and the "causes" which preceded those conditions. The difficulty with this neurological approach is that the causes of saying "No, thank you" ultimately lie outside, not inside, the organism.[7] Consequently, Skinner is extremely skeptical about the usefulness of neurophysiological findings in predicting and controlling human behavior. Of course, this attitude is to be

5. B. F. Skinner, *The Behavior of Organisms*, p. 44.
6. Skinner, *Science and Human Behavior*, p. 28.
7. *Ibid.*

expected since his psychology is based on the assumption that man's behavior is a function of external variables.[8] By his definition of behavior the so-called inner causes, physical or mental, become unnecessary for a scientific investigation of behavior.

Mental States The usual practice among laymen and perhaps some psychologists is to explain the behavior of others by attributing it to certain mental or emotional conditions. Thus, John is said to play the piano well because he has musical ability or Bob is said to smoke a great deal because he has a smoking habit. But if "having musical ability" means "playing the piano well" and "having a smoking habit" is equivalent by definition to "smoking a great deal," do these statements explain anything at all? Skinner inquires:

> To what extent is it helpful to be told, "He drinks because he is thirsty?" If to be thirsty means nothing more than to have a tendency to drink, this is mere redundancy. If it means that he drinks because of a state of thirst, an inner causal event is invoked. If this state is purely inferential—if no dimensions are assigned to it which would make direct observation possible—it cannot serve as an explanation. But if it has physiological or psychic properties, what role can it play in a science of behavior?[9]

In short, the inner causes, whether they are intentions, ambitions, hunger, fatigue, or thirst, are not explanatory concepts, because they are either tautologies or they are not immediately observable. Therefore, they are only, in Skinner's phrase, "explanatory fictions!"

In opposing the use of inner states as explanations of observable behavior, Skinner carefully points out that he does not deny the existence of inner states, because "an adequate science of human behavior must consider events taking place within the skin of the organism . . . as part of behavior

8. Skinner, *The Behavior of Organisms,* p. 44.
9. Skinner, *Science and Human Behavior,* p. 33.

itself."[10] But he cautions us against treating inner states as having a special nature to be known by special methods, for "the skin is not that important as a boundary. Private and public events both have the same kinds of physical dimensions."[11] In other words, we must deal with events taking place inside and outside of the skin of the organism in exactly the same way. But it seems to me that to demand that the method used in studying the observable events be applied to the investigation of inner states is to suggest that we disregard the latter. And if inner states are as much a part of human behavior as overt responses, how could they be considered irrelevant in a scientific analysis of man's behavior?

The Value of Theories

By now it should be clear that for Skinner the only proper role for psychology is to analyze human behavior by accurately *describing* the conditions under which responses occur. He stubbornly insists that in carrying out such a scientific inquiry we should be concerned with reporting directly observable variables without theorizing about them. Skinner is adamantly antagonistic to theories (1) which refer to "any explanation of an observed fact which appeals to events taking place somewhere else, at some other level of observation, described in different terms, and measured, if at all, in different dimensions," and (2) in which "explanatory events are not directly observed. . . ."[12] He is opposed to the first kind of theory because it contains either physiological or mentalistic expressions, thereby unobservable inner states. The second type of theory is unacceptable to Skinner because it stresses the formulation and testing of hypotheses based on postulates, constructs, or other theoretical entities without any directly observable referents. He goes on to point out that

10. Skinner, "Behaviorism at Fifty," p. 84.
11. B. F. Skinner, "Are Theories of Learning Necessary?" *Psychological Review*, Vol. 57, No. 4, July, 1950, p. 193.
12. *Ibid.*, pp. 193–194.

the emphasis we place on validating hypotheses is futile and extravagant because the result of scientific investigation, whether it is descriptive or an effort to confirm a hypothesis, is a described functional relationship demonstrated in data. Describing his own approach to scientific investigation he wrote:

> I never faced a problem which was more than the eternal problem of finding order. I never attacked a problem by constructing a Hypothesis. I never deduced theorems or submitted them to Experimental Check. So far as I can see, I had no preconceived Mode of behavior—certainly not a physiological or mentalistic one, and I believe not a conceptual one. . . . Of course, I was working on a basic assumption—that there was order in behavior if I could only discover it—but such an assumption is not to be confused with the hypothesis of deductive theory. It is also true that I exercised a certain selection of facts, not because of relevance to theory but because one fact was more orderly than another. If I engaged in experimental design at all, it was simply to complete or extend some evidence of order already observed.[13]

Because the ends sought by both theoretical and descriptive investigations are the same, the only point at issue is which method of investigation more efficiently directs the inquiry. Skinner is firmly convinced that purely behavioral definitions of terms are much more efficient and advantageous than conceptual definitions, for they avoid the difficulty of explaining how mental causes bring about physical effects or vice versa.

Despite his strong antitheoretical stance, Skinner is not opposed to the kind of theory which summarizes lawful relationships among the collected data.[14] Consequently, for Skinner, one of the steps in conducting a scientific inquiry, after lawful relationships have been discovered and an appreciable quantity of data collected, is to represent the data in the form of a shorthand summary, using a minimal number of

13. B. F. Skinner, "A Case History in Scientific Method," *Psychology: A Study of Science*, S. Koch, ed., Vol. II, p. 369.
14. Skinner, "Theories of Learning," pp. 215–216.

terms and mathematical representation. He thinks that this sort of theoretical construction is legitimate for it gives us greater generality than a mere collection of individual facts. Indeed, it is curious that in spite of his overwhelmingly descriptive approach to psychology, he maintains that "science is more than mere description of events as they occur. . . . It is an attempt to discover order, to show that certain events stand in lawful relations to other events."[15] Skinner is clearly consistent with this view when he claims that he only looks "for lawful process in the behavior of the intact organism,"[16] and nothing more.

Thus Skinner contends that the objective order in the behavior of an organism can be discovered as it exists apart from man's judgment and interpretation. He further asserts that with sufficient observation of responses the order becomes self-evident, for once the data are in order the theories tend to become unnecessary. In other words, a set of observation statements about some aspect of human behavior will reveal an inherent and objective order without having the observer interpret or arrange the data according to some conceptual scheme—which is not itself a product of observation.

METHODOLOGICAL BEHAVIORISM AND THE VERIFIABILITY PRINCIPLE

Skinner's view of science makes it abundantly clear that methodological behaviorism as a behavioral science is founded on the verifiability principle. In brief, this principle asserts that for any factual statement to be meaningful, it must be empirically verifiable. Hence, all statements, psychological or otherwise, which purport to inform us about matters of fact must be publicly verifiable. But what does the term *verifiable* mean? Originally its supporters, logical positivists, interpreted *verification* to mean conclusive verification, which

15. Skinner, *Science and Human Behavior*, p. 6.
16. Skinner, "Scientific Method," p. 362.

entails perception (direct and immediate observation) of whatever is being verified. According to this interpretation all statements about matters of fact must have physical dimensions which are directly observable. Mentalistic and neurophysiological terms as well as reports of private experiences would not, of course, meet this requirement. Therefore, they are not accepted as legitimate parts of a scientific explanation. However, in recent years a much broader interpretation has been given to the principle, so that the term *verifiable* is now generally understood as indirect verification or empirical confirmation, which requires that empirical statements must be confirmable by competent observers. That is, "to say that a statement is empirically *confirmable* is to say that possible observations can be described that would, if they were made, bestow some degree of probability on the statement."[17] In this broader interpretation of the principle the emphasis falls more on the consequence of a statement. For example, if we say that "when a rat is deprived of food until it reaches 85 percent of its normal body weight, there will be a corresponding increase in tension within the rat and this increase will motivate the organism to act in a certain way so as to reduce tension and restore equilibrium," this statement can be empirically confirmed if the rat did behave as predicted following food deprivation. However, an assertion of this type is never conclusively verifiable, because the terms *tension, equilibrium,* and *motivated* are not amenable to direct observation. But within the context of the broader conception of the verifiability principle, inference and constructs may become useful parts of scientific inquiry. It is important to note here that unless *verifiability* is understood as empirical confirmation it would not have been possible to formulate even the laws of gravitation, thermodynamics, and heredity, for we can only observe the consequences of the assumed existence of gravitation, thermodynamics, and genes.

Now, returning to Skinner's position, from all he has said about the proper subject matter and method of psychology,

17. Arthur Pap, *An Introduction to the Philosophy of Science,* p. 17.

there is little doubt that he stands firmly committed to the original version of the verifiability principle. And because he demands all factual statements to be conclusively verifiable, he has no alternative but to dismiss everything except immediately observable facts as irrelevant in a science of behavior. It is for this same reason that Skinner sees human behavior as a series of individual responses which are related to each other in time only. And on the same grounds he maintains that statements about evidently meaningful private and mental experiences are nothing more than explanatory fictions.

ANALYTIC BEHAVIORISM AND THE IDENTITY THEORY OF MIND

Before we move on to the overall evaluation of Skinner's methodological (or descriptive) behaviorism we need to examine analytic behaviorism and the identity theory of mind, because they represent the two most recent approaches to psychology and the mind-body problem, and also because some of their features are easily confused with certain tenets of the Skinnerean point of view.

Analytic Behaviorism

Philosophically, methodological behaviorism represents a particular point of view regarding the proper subject matter and method for psychology as an empirical science. As such it does not necessarily entail materialism, the point of view that everything in the universe, including the mind, is reducible to, and explainable in terms of, matter and motion. In other words, it is logically possible for someone to believe in the substantive view of mind and yet insist that the only proper way for studying man's mental functions is in terms of immediately observable responses. He may even admit that there are mental inner states which cannot be studied empirically. Methodological behaviorism as a point of view about the methodology of psychology is consistent, or rather is not inconsistent, with dualistic interactionism or the substantive view of the mind. Actually, however, no advocate of the substantive view of the mind is likely to be a methodological behaviorist, because as a rule individuals who think of the mind as an unextended substance are not likely to find the verifiability principle very congenial to their philosophical perspective. In any event, Skinner's own position is materialistic in that he leaves no room in his psychology for anything mental.[18]

Analytic behaviorism is unlike methodological behaviorism in that it is unconcerned with the methodological question. It addresses itself primarily to the question of the translatability of psychological terms into physicalistic propositions. According to one of its outstanding proponents, analytic behaviorism asserts that

> all psychological statements which are meaningful, that is to say, which are in principle verifiable, are translatable into propositions which do not involve psychological concepts, but only the concepts of physics. The propositions of psychology are consequently physicalistic propositions. Psychology is an integral part of physics.[19]

To put this differently, all psychological terms are reducible to the thing-language and hence finally to observable thing-predicates,[20] so that psychological statements can be regarded as statements about the physical processes in the body of the organism in question. Hence, psychological constructs are

18. Skinner, "Behaviorism at Fifty," p. 106.
19. Carl G. Hempel, "The Logical Analysis of Psychology," *Readings in Philosophical Analysis*, Herbert Feigl and Wilfred Sellars, eds., p. 378. In clarifying the use of the term *physics,* Carnap remarks: "By 'physics' we wish to mean, not the system of currently known physical laws, but rather the science characterized by a mode of concept formation which traces every concept back to state-coordinates, that is, to systematic assignments of numbers to space-time points." Rudolf Carnap, "Psychology in Physical Language," George Schick, trans., *Logical Positivism,* A. J. Ayer, ed., p. 197.
20. Rudolf Carnap, "Logical Foundations of the Unity of Science," *Readings in Philosophical Analysis*, Herbert Feigl and Wilfred Sellars, eds., p. 416.

seen as "abbreviations of physicalistic statements."[21] This implies that we should be able to restate psychological propositions by using only the terms which refer to specific sense data, e.g., *cold, hot, hard,* or *soft.* Fundamentally, analytic behaviorism is a form of materialism in which the primary concern lies in the reduction of psychological language into the language of physics.

The Identity Theory of Mind

In contrast to analytic behaviorism, the identity theory of mind, though materialistic, denies that all significant psychological propositions can be translated into physicalistic expressions, because the languages of psychology and physics have two widely different kinds of meaning. But it does say that the term *mind* is another way of talking about very complex neural processes taking place within the central nervous system. According to Herbert Feigl, "The states of direct experience which conscious human beings "live through," and those which we confidently ascribe to some of the higher animals, are identical with certain (presumably configuration) aspects of the neural processes in those organisms."[22] In short, the mental states we experience can be described in both psychological and neurophysiological terms, which have different meanings. Both, however, describe neural processes in the sense in which "lightning" and "exchange of electric currents between two layers of ionized cloud" refer to one and the same physical event. When we see a flash of lightning, we do not experience lightning and another occurrence called "exchange of electric currents between two layers of ionized cloud," for the referent of these expressions is the same. An identity theorist, J.J.C. Smart wrote:

21. Hempel, "Logical Analysis," p. 381.
22. Herbert Feigl, "The 'Mental' and the 'Physical,'" *Minnesota Studies in the Philosophy of Science*, Vol. II, *Concepts, Theories and the Mind-Body Problem*, Herbert Feigl, Michael Scrivin, and Grover Maxwell, eds., p. 446.

> When I say that a sensation is a brain process or that lightning is an electric discharge, I am using "is" in the sense of strict identity. . . . When I say that a sensation is a brain process or that lightning is an electric discharge I do not mean that the sensation is somehow spatially or temporally continuous with the brain process or that the lightning is just spatially or temporally continuous with the discharge.[23]

However, the logic of a "sensation statement" is not the same as that of a "brain-process statement," because the fact that a single process, say thinking, can be described in both psychological as well as neurological terms should be "interpreted as a correlation of two reports expressed in terms of two different languages about an identical event . . . just as we should expect a report of a laboratory experiment written by a student in French to correspond, statement for statement, with a report of the same experiment written by a student in English, so with the reports of this brain experiment, one written in physical language and the other in the language of immediacy."[24] In one sense the advocates of the identity theory are like analytic behaviorists in that they are concerned with forms of linguistic expressions and their relationships. But basically the identity theorists are not linguistic philosophers, because they are ultimately interested in nonlinguistic phenomena, namely, the neurophysiological processes in man. Because they maintain that psychological statements do have unique meanings of their own, they can consistently argue that a science of behavior does not need to be a branch of either biology or physics.

CONCLUDING COMMENTS

In defending the view that a science of behavior must remain purely descriptive and atheoretical, Skinner assumes

---

23. J. J. C. Smart, "Sensations and Brain Processes," *The Philosophical Review*, Vol. LXVIII, No. 2, 1959, p. 145.
24. Stephen C. Pepper, "A Neural-Identity Theory of Mind," *Dimensions of Mind*, Sidney Hook, ed., p. 46.

that objective order and lawfulness of the behavior of organisms are discoverable if we make sufficient observations of specific responses as they occur. If one accepts this premise, he has no need for theorizing; nor does he have to be concerned about inner states, physical or mental. What Skinner does not seem to realize is that empirical observation is almost never a matter of just "seeing," for we always "see" events or objects as this or that. Consequently, when we say that we heard a sour note at a concert, we are not implying that we first perceived (observed) a tone, which we later judged (interpreted) as being sour. Quite to the contrary, we do hear a sour note, because we perceive the tone in relation to other tones as well as our own mental picture of what that particular piece of music should sound like. Observation which does not contain any degree of interpretive judgment is impossible. If it were possible, there would not be any difference between Skinner and Guthrie, for both men are strong proponents of a strictly descriptive and atheoretical science of behavior; they could observe the order in human behavior as it exists apart from the observer's bias and interpretation. Yet, Skinner claims that learning usually requires more than one pairing of a response and a reinforcer, while Guthrie attaches little significance to reinforcement, because he maintains that learning takes place at the first pairing of a stimulus and a response. Whose account accurately describes the order in human behavior as it exists independently of man's judgment? This, of course, is an unanswerable question since we cannot observe (know) things as they are in themselves. Skinner is naive if he seriously believes that pure observation of world phenomena is possible, for, "there is more to 'seeing' than meets the eyeball. And there is much more to scientific observation than merely standing alert with sense organs 'at the ready,' because it is all interest-directed and context-dependent."[25] Hence, the only way in which two individuals with different philo-

---

25. Norwood Russell Hanson, "Observation and Interpretation," *Philosophy of Science Today*, Sidney Morgenbesser, ed., p. 91.

sophical and theoretical perspectives can be said to make the same observation is in describing their perceptions in terms of immediate sense data. In other words, to observe is not to have a mass of sense data but to have an experience. Therefore, "slicing the incoming signals of sensation from an appreciating of the significance of these signals would destroy what we know as scientific observation."[26]

NEUROLOGY AND EDUCATION

Skinner observes correctly that psychological study of human behavior is possible without relying on information concerning neurophysiological processes which go on within the behaving organism. He is also right in arguing that knowledge about man's behavior cannot be obtained by studying neurology or physiology alone. But he grossly underestimates the significant contribution neurology and physiology can make to our understanding of human behavior when he insists that only external and directly observable responses can give us reliable psychological knowledge.

Notwithstanding Skinner's doubts about the worth of neurological findings in the study of human behavior, there has been some interesting and important progress made in this area. Many significant studies have been made about the neurological bases of readiness, reinforcement, and other aspects of the learning process. Of these, one of the most fascinating is the recent work related to memory storage, in particular the organic (anatomical) changes brought about by learning experiences. Indeed, the results of these investigations may have some far-reaching ramifications for education. For example, Karl H. Pribram reports that a group of investigators found that chemical changes produced in rats by different kinds and varying amounts of experience were correlated with changes in the thickness of the cerebral cortex

---

26. *Ibid.,* p. 89.

involved.[27] Since nerve cells do not grow in number, the thickening change was attributed to increased branching of the nerve-fibers. It was also learned that different areas of the brain were affected by different kinds of exercises and that the mechanisms serving learning and retention were controlled by different regions of the brain cortex. In Pribram's own words:

> Lesions of the brain cortex (made with aluminum hydroxide crea), which caused marked disturbance of the electrical record, *impede learning* some five-fold but *leave intact retention* of solutions to problems. Conversely, removal of the same cortical tissue have little effect on the acquisition of new but related problem-solutions during any one training session; however, recall of the previous day's performances is severely restricted.[28]

David Krech made a similar discovery when he studied two groups of rats taken from two different environments. He found that the brains of rats from the enriched environment (an environment with many rat toys, ladders, and levers for various activities) had heavier and thicker cortices, better blood supplies, larger brain cells, and increased activity of two brain enzymes, acetylcholinesterase and cholinesterase, than did the brains of rats taken from the environment which did not have the same enriching elements.[29] The altered physical characteristics of the rats from the enriched environment were thought to be one of the consequences of having more stored memories than did their counterparts from less enriched surroundings. With further understanding of the neurophysiological basis of learning it may be possible in the future to make learning and/or unlearning more efficient by affecting man's brains by chemical (e.g., drugs) or electrical

27. Karl H. Pribram, "Neurological Notes on the Art of Educating," *Theories of Learning,* The Sixty-Third Yearbook of the National Society for the Study of Education, Ernest Hilgard, ed., p. 86.
28. *Ibid.,* p. 87.
29. David Krech, "Psychoneurobiochemeducation," *Phi Delta Kappan,* March, 1969. pp. 371–373. For an interesting discussion of the physical control of man's mental processes see *Behavior Control* by Perry London (New York: Harper and Row, 1969).

means. However, interestingly enough Krech indicates that "manipulating the educational and psychological environment is a more effective way of inducing long-lasting brain change than direct administration of drugs."[30]

José M.R. Delgado, professor of Physiology at Yale University, and a specialist in the study of primate and human behavior through electrical and chemical stimulation of the brain, agrees with Krech in stating that individual experiences, e.g., learning experiences, can lead to measurable changes in chemistry and anatomy of the brain.[31] He emphasizes the importance of individual experiences and social variables in determining human and certain primate behavior by citing experiments with monkeys and human subjects. In one experiment, the state of hostility was induced in male monkeys through the electrical stimulation of several structures in the brain. These monkeys were said to have occupied high social and leadership positions in several colonies, which constituted autocratic societies. In this experiment the stimulated monkeys attacked only those males who represented a challenge to their authority suggesting that the monkeys' previous experiences were important factors in determining the direction of the intragroup aggression.[32] In the experiments involving human subjects who were committed to a ward for the criminally insane, assaultative behavior was induced in the subjects by radio stimulation of the right amygdala of the brain. Again the aggressive acts of the subjects were not directed to the persons interviewing them but to nearby objects and to the wall, thus indicating their awareness of the social position of the interviewers. On the basis of these and other studies, Delgado holds that the expression of mental and/or emotional states induced by electrical stimulation of the brain is dependent on the social setting and that understanding of human behavior and its

30. *Ibid.,* p. 373.
31. José M. R. Delgado, *Physical Control of the Mind,* p. 52.
32. For this and other related discussions refer to Chapter 14, "Hell and Heaven within the Brain," in *Physical Control of the Mind.*

alterations requires knowledge of both sociology and neurophysiology.

In his attempt to reproduce the sort of psychological environment which led to the already-mentioned chemical and anatomical changes in the rat brain, Krech had many groups of rats living in several different surroundings. Later the rats were dissected and their brains examined. Krech summarizes his findings as follows:

> *First:* Sheer exercise or physical activity alone is not at all effective in developing the brain. A physical training director seems not to be an adequate substitute for a teacher.
>
> *Second:* Varied visual stimulation, or indeed any kind of visual stimulation, is neither necessary nor sufficient to develop the brain, as we were able to demonstrate by using rats blinded at weaning age.
>
> *Third:* Handling, or taming, or petting is also without effect in developing the growing rat's brain. Love is Not Enough.
>
> *Fourth:* The presence of a brother rat in our intellectually deprived rat's cage helps him not a whit. *Bruderschaft* is not enough.
>
> *Fifth:* Teaching the rat to press levers for food—that and only that—seems to help somewhat, but only minimally. Not every problem-set will do, either.[33]

Curiously enough, the only variable that was effective in bringing about the organic changes in the rat's brain was "freedom to roam around in a large object-filled space."[34] To Krech these data suggested that there may be what he calls *"species-specific enrichment experiences."*[35] That is, individual species of organisms may have a set of specific experiences which maximally develop their brains. Hence, what is effective in developing rat brains will not necessarily be useful to man. What then would be some species-specific enrichment experiences for children? Though there is not yet a definitive

33. Krech, "Psychoneurobiochemeducation," p. 373.
34. *Ibid.*
35. *Ibid.*

answer to the question, Krech speculates that the cognitive activities in learning and using a language may be related to such experiences.[36] Certainly it is not unreasonable to suppose that we might find biochemical boosters and inhibitors for different kinds of abilities, memories, or even personality traits. But the task of educating the child will not be in the hands of any single group of people, whether psychologists or neurologists, because as Krech said, "[it] will come to rest in the knowledge and skills of the biochemist, and pharmacologist, and neurologist, and psychologists, and educator. And there will be a new expert abroad in the land—the psychoneurobiochemeducator."[37]

While it is true that much of what Krech has said about "species-specific enrichment experiences" are no more than educated guesses, there are good grounds for insisting that in whatever approach we take in the study of human learning, the education of the child requires all the wisdom and skills we can muster from every field of human knowledge.

MENTAL STATES AND PRIVATE EXPERIENCES

Skinner is at least partially correct in pointing out that statements such as "He smokes a great deal because he has the smoking habit," and "He plays the piano well because he has musical ability" do not explain anything. Because if, by definition, "the smoking habit" and "having musical ability" imply "smoking a great deal" and "playing the piano well," respectively, they are only circular or redundant statements. But Skinner is mistaken if he takes a dispositional statement such as "He drinks because he is thirsty" as a redundant statement in the same sense in which the above mentioned statements are circular. Let me clarify this point further. All men have the capacity to become thirsty or to have a tendency to drink. But a tendency to drink can be caused by many variables. We can come to have a tendency to drink

36. *Ibid.*, p. 374.
37. *Ibid.*

because of a twenty-mile hike without any water, or our disposition to drink can be induced by a certain type of brain operation. And still we can be made to drink by threats or rewards. Moreover, when we offer "He drinks because he is thirsty" as an explanation of a particular individual's behavior, it is almost always given within a specific context in which information about relevant factors is given. That is, in the context of a twenty-mile hike the statement, "He drinks because he is thirsty," would probably mean, "He went on a twenty-mile hike when the temperature was 105° F without any water, and these conditions induced his disposition to drink; therefore he drank a lot of water." No doubt additional physiological explanations can be given. The main point here is that whenever we say, "He drinks because he is thirsty," as an explanation we usually have information about the variables which led to the individual's tendency to drink at that particular time and place. The context will also tell us something about the factors which had nothing to do with the act in question. In other words, if a person drinks because he became thirsty as a result of taking a twenty-mile hike, we would know with reasonable certainty that his act of drinking was not caused by a threat of some sort. The point that Skinner misses in his discussion is the fact that no one ever offers "He drinks because he is thirsty" as an explanation without providing at least some additional information, directly or contextually. Michael Scriven made a similar observation when he remarked:

> Even if "to be thirsty means nothing more than to have a tendency to drink" it is by no means merely redundant to be told that on this occasion he drank because of that tendency rather than under compulsion or because of a tendency to eat or etc. To have a tendency is to have a certain disposition, and everyone has some disposition to drink, but it is not always that disposition which explains our drinking. When we are satiated, for example, we have a short term disposition not to drink; and, in such a case, the statement that we drank because we were thirsty would not, even on Skinner's first analysis, be redundant; it would be false. . . . [Hence] to chastise the ordinary explanations of

individual events by reference to dispositions, on the grounds that some explanations of patterns of behavior by reference to dispositions are redundant, is manifestly unfair.[38]

There is no doubt that private experiences and neurophysiological states are not directly observable, therefore what we say about them is subject to error and misunderstanding. But statements about observable events too are fallible, perhaps to a lesser degree. Therefore,

> to maintain that planning, deliberating, preference, choice, volition, pleasure, pain, displeasure, love, hatred, . . . etc. are not among the causal factors which determine human behavior, is to fly in the face of the commonest of evidence, or else to deviate in a strange and unjustifiable way from the ordinary use of language. The task is neither to repudiate these obvious facts, nor to rule out this manner of describing them. The task is rather to analyze the logical status of this sort of description in its relation to behavioral and/or neurophysiological descriptions.[39]

The mental and the neurophysiological states of other persons are clearly not verifiable in any conclusive sense. But occurrences of such states are empirically confirmable. In other words, since each of us can verify the occurrence of certain mental states within us we can empirically confirm or disconfirm that a particular mental state has or has not taken place in another person by the use of analogical argument (e.g., when I am in a sad mood there are observable symptoms X, Y, and Z; when I observe another person exhibiting these outward symptoms I can reasonably say that he is in a sad mood). It is logically impossible for us to conclusively verify another person's toothache, for we would have to perceive that

---

38. Michael Scriven, "A Study of Radical Behaviorism," *Minnesota Studies in the Philosophy of Science,* Vol. I, *The Foundations of Science and the Concepts of Psychology and Psychoanalysis,* Herbert Feigl and Michael Scriven, eds., p. 121. Here Scriven is talking about Skinner's analysis of "the smoking habit," and "has musical ability" as explanations of "smoking a great deal" and "playing the piano well," respectively. See Skinner's *Science and Human Behavior,* pp. 31–33.
39. Feigl, "Mental and Physical," p. 389.

person's toothache. But if we perceive another man's toothache, it becomes ours, hence we have not verified the toothache in question. Yet, if we have reliable information about the kinds of overt symptoms usually associated with "having a toothache," it is possible to confirm whether the person in question has a toothache. This is the way we usually communicate with others.

An adequate science of behavior must deal with events taking place both inside and outside of the behaving organism. This does not mean that inner happenings should be known in the same way we come to know the observable responses. To demand that the "inner states" be known as we know the external, immediately observable, variables is to dismiss the former as being useless without sufficient warrant. Benjamin Wolman reminds us, "the task of scientific inquiry is to seek truth, be it visible and observable or private. If there are private events, we must study them. We shall study them as objectively as possible. . . . Science has to study things as they are and cannot reject things because they do not fit into one's intellectual preference or modes of thinking."[40] But Skinner does reject inner states, mental and physical, because they do not fit into his particular mode of thinking, i.e., inner states are not conclusively verifiable. In one sense Skinner is similar to a man who is looking for his ring under the street lamp, because there is more light there than in the dark alley where he lost the ring.

IS A PURELY DESCRIPTIVE SCIENCE OF BEHAVIOR POSSIBLE?

After hearing so much about the antitheoretical attitude and the descriptive approach to science it is something of a surprise to learn that Skinner thinks of science as "more than mere description of events as they occur."[41] But he is correct

40. Benjamin B. Wolman, "Toward a Science of Psychological Science," *Scientific Psychology*, Benjamin B. Wolman, ed., p. 12.
41. Skinner, *Science and Human Behavior*, p. 6.

in regarding science as "an attempt to discover order, to show that certain events stand in lawful relations to other events."[42] Contrary to Skinner's own assumption, discovering such order and lawfulness requires more than just a pile of facts, because facts alone do not reveal order. In brief, facts do not speak for themselves! We must interpret the data and bridge gaps in our observation with constructs (theoretical entities) and postulates. Drawing inferences and testing hypotheses are other essential aspects of an empirical science.

Scientific explanations are never absolutely true nor are they always conclusively verifiable. At best they are empirically confirmed statements about probable events. Even the laws in physics, chemistry, and astronomy are accepted as highly confirmed hypotheses, which "are all *universal* propositions, stating that under specified conditions such and such happens *always and everywhere*."[43] Within this conception of science, constructs or the terms referring to inferred states or processes are useful tools, in so far as they have observable consequences, which help us to explain a phenomenon under investigation. Theoretical constructs such as *motive, drive, ego,* etc. are said to exist when their specified consequences eventuate. The constructs, therefore, need not be directly observable as long as they have observable effects. And we should regard them as "real in such-and-such a respect, but unreal . . . in such-and-such another respect."[44] Constructs may not only be used as a legitimate part of scientific explanation but they are often necessary in explaining why certain phenomena take place. Even Skinner himself has not been successful in avoiding terms which have no observable referents. For example, it is usually assumed that the term *conditioning* merely describes a particular kind of relationship between stimulus and responses and this applies to both classical and operant conditioning. But does the term refer to a directly observable stimulus-response relationship? The

42. *Ibid.*
43. Pap, *Philosophy of Science*, p. 17.
44. Scrivin, *Radical Behaviorism*, p. 117.

answer is a resounding no, for all we can "see" directly in a conditioning process is that one event merely follows another. Hence, something more than mere temporal sequence is tacitly presupposed, for the term *conditioning* is not applied to all instances of one behavioral event following another. That is, if a person always twitches his nose before scratching his head we would not necessarily say that the scratching was a conditioned response to twitching unless the association between them is of a certain kind. Such a relationship implies that a stimulus "can make a response happen." Skinner himself uses the term *reinforcement* to mean that which *increases* the probability of a response. Indeed, there are many situations in which a response following a stimulus would not be called either conditioning or reinforcement. Without assuming some sort of a connection, neurological or otherwise, between stimulus and response the concept of conditioning would not be distinguishable from mere temporal sequence.

Another example of Skinner's inability to follow his own methodological dictum is his view of the Law of Effect. In his article "Are Theories of Learning Necessary?" Skinner states that, "anyone who has seen such a demonstration knows that the Law of Effect is no theory."[45] He is, of course, referring to those situations in which a reinforcing event following a response increases the probability of that response. What Skinner is suggesting is that the expression "Law of Effect" *does* stand for a directly observable variable, i.e., the event in which a reinforcer *does in fact increase* the probability of that response. However, Skinner cannot see such an event. What he does observe is an event following another event. But in what way does this observation differ from Newton's observation of a falling apple? Is not the Law of Effect or the notion of reinforcement as much of a theoretical concept as the term *gravitation?* The difficulty with Skinner's position is that any system which claims to be based solely on the

45. Skinner, "Theories of Learning," p. 200.

observation of specific responses and the frequency of their occurrence can only generalize about the probability of a particular response on the basis of the observation of prior occurrences. Hence, without making other assumptions we cannot formulate a law(s) covering all responses and their reinforcers. In quoting Henri Poincaré, a nineteenth-century French mathematical physicist, Benjamin Wolman reminds us that "'pure' empiricism does not make science more rigorous; rather it makes it less adequate. A mere collection of facts is no more a science than a pile of bricks is a house."[46]

A basic flaw of Skinner's methodological behaviorism lies in its inability to explain adequately such complex phases of man's behavior as language learning, abstract thinking, and other high level cognitive processes. This weakness is due primarily to the behaviorists' failure to distinguish conclusive verification from empirical confirmation as the criterion of meaning. Once the verifiability principle had been interpreted so narrowly it was unavoidable that methodological behaviorists would disregard mental processes and neurophysiological conditions as irrelevant. In a sense methodological behaviorists can be likened to Zeno and Parmenides who denied man's immediate experience of motion, because the concept did not fit into their scheme of logic and assumptions. What Skinnereans need to do is to broaden their conception of verification and also to "strengthen its [methodological behaviorism's] core by admitting the contributions which other disciplines within psychology are making and by usefully incorporating and improving them whenever they are relevant."[47] As Pribram continues,

the problem to which operant behaviorism is addressed is reinforcement. Reinforcement is a central problem in psychology "by whatever name it is called: outcome, consequence, law of effect, feedback, stamping in, etc." Thus the demand for a sophisticated

46. Wolman, "Psychological Science," p. 11.
47. Karl H. Pribram, "Comment," *Explanation in the Behavioral Sciences*, Robert Borger and Frank Cioffi, eds., Cambridge, The University Press, 1970, p. 380.

operant behaviorism pervades psychology. But the converse also holds or should hold—psychology must pervade operant behaviorism if either is to remain viable.[48]

Before closing this chapter we should make some brief comments about analytic behaviorism and the identity theory of mind. There is much that we can say about the relative merits of the linguistic approach analytic behaviorism takes in dealing with the mind-body problem and psychology. But for our purpose, it is enough to point out that translation of a rather simple statement such as "I am hungry" into a set of physicalistic expressions is difficult, but possible. However, I have the gravest doubts about the possibility of translating "I accept the verifiability principle" or other statements about beliefs into physicalistic propositions "pointing" only to the properties of observable things.

As to the identity theory, all of its proponents agree that for every mental state there is a corresponding physical state, and vice versa. They also concur that such correlation between the mental and the physical is possible, because they happen to be one and the same. Yet, there is no common view regarding the status of mentalistic expressions. For instance, Feigl argues that mental states have causal efficacy (see n. 39) and that mentalistic terms represent "the directly experienced qualia [or raw-feelings] and configurations [which] are the realities-in-themselves that are denoted by the neurophysiological descriptions."[49] But if this is true, Feigl becomes an unusual interactionist in that he has given the mind its own existence. Unlike Feigl, Smart sees the mentalistic language as just another way of talking about the brain process. To be sure it is a vague, ambiguous, and imprecise way. But this position makes Smart's version of identity theory a double language theory, which asserts that there are two widely different languages for describing a single physical reality.

One of the most often raised objections against the "double

48. *Ibid.*
49. Feigl, "Mental and Physical," p. 457.

language version" of the identity theory is that we do not have sufficient evidence to support the notion that the mental and the physical are indeed one and the same. The critics insist that we only have evidence to justify the claim that there is a correlation or concomitant change in conditions between the mind and the body. That is, the fact that the statement "I have a headache" is accompanied by certain physical changes within the organism in question does not necessarily mean that they are in fact referring to a single physical process. The critics go on to point out that according to the principle of the identity of indiscernables, objects which appear to be different from each other are in fact identical if both or all of them have exactly the same properties. Conversely, if objects are identical, they have the same properties. Hence, "the fiftieth state of the United States" is identical with "Hawaii," because they have exactly the same set of properties. But the critics contend that the identity theory has not been able to show that the properties of the mental processes are in fact identical with those of the physical phenomena going on within the organism. They further argue that not all physical conditions have corresponding mental states. Moreover, the terms used in describing mental states cannot properly be used to describe physical states. For example, we may speak of *fading* memory, *nagging* headache, *dim* perception, etc., but we do not say that our neurological processes are fading or that we have nagging physiological conditions. Hence, the mental and the physical processes are basically different from each other.

To this objection some identity theorists may reply by saying that in claiming that the mental and physical are identical, and that they are not two separate processes, mental and physical, which turn out to have the same set of properties, but that there is only one kind of reality, which is physical throughout. Therefore, mentalistic and physicalistic expressions describe different aspects of the same process from different points of view. That is, mentalistic statements may be considered as introspective reports about certain physical processes taking place within the observer, whereas physicalistic propositions may be thought of as descriptive (and objective) statements about certain physical phenomena. It would seem that this kind of identity theory would have strong appeal to many, for today there are enough studies in physiological psychology, neurology, biochemistry, and genetics which present some very convincing data to suggest that man, like other animals, is a physical entity and that the processes going on within him are very complex but still physical in nature. This view does not, of course, imply that we can make no distinction between the mental and the physical, for certain aspects of the physical processes may be called mental and others physical. It seems to me that whether we conceive the mind to be a pattern of responses, or a quality of action, or a set of dispositions, it is difficult, if not impossible, to deny that all of our overt actions are outer manifestations of extremely complex neurophysiological processes going on within us. Hence, I cannot help thinking that accurate knowledge of these processes will add immeasurably to our understanding of human behavior and the means of influencing it.

As we have seen in Chapters 4 and 5 Skinner regards all mentalistic terms in psychology as explanatory fictions. Yet, there are others who claim that understanding, insight, intentions, motives, and emotions are central to the study and improvement of teaching-learning processes. Indeed, most educators and psychologists as well as philosophers would agree that in teaching we should be concerned with influencing children's overt actions as well as their attitudes and beliefs. Hence, assertions about the nature and significance of mental processes and emotions should not be simply explained, or rather argued away. On the contrary, they deserve a careful study and evaluation. Therefore, we shall now turn to an examination of the cognitive views on teaching and learning and their underlying concept of the mind.

BIBLIOGRAPHY

Books

Carnap, Rudolf, "Logical Foundations of the Unity of Science," *Readings in Philosophical Analysis,* Herbert Feigl and Wilfred Sellars, eds. New York: Appleton-Century-Crofts, Inc., 1949.

——— "Psychology in Physical Language," George Schick, trans., *Logical Positivism,* A. J. Ayer, ed. New York: The Free Press, 1959.

Delgado, José M.R., *Physical Control of the Mind.* New York: Harper and Row, Publishers, 1969.

Feigl, Herbert, "The 'Mental' and the 'Physical'," *Minnesota Studies in the Philosophy of Science,* Vol. II, *Concepts, Theories and the Mind-Body Problem,* Herbert Feigl, Michael Scrivin, and Grover Maxwell, eds. Minneapolis: University of Minnesota Press, 1958.

Hempel, Carl G., "The Logical Analysis of Psychology," *Readings in Philosophical Analysis,* Herbert Feigl and Wilfred Sellars, eds. New York: Appleton-Century-Crofts, Inc., 1949.

Hanson, Norwood Russell, "Observation and Interpretation," *Philosophy of Science Today,* Sidney Morgenbesser, ed. New York: Basic Books, Inc. 1967.

Pap, Arthur, *An Introduction to the Philosophy of Science.* New York: The Free Press of Glenco, 1962.

Pepper, Stephen, "A Neural-Identity Theory of Mind," *Dimensions of Mind,* Sidney Hook, ed. New York: New York University Press, 1960.

Pribram, Karl H., "Comment," *Explanations in the Behavioral Sciences,* Robert Borger and Frank Cioffi, eds. Cambridge: The University Press, 1970.

——— "Neurological Notes on the Art of Educating," *Theories of Learning,* The Sixty-Third Yearbook of the National Society for the Study of Education, Ernest Hilgard, ed. Chicago: The University of Chicago Press, 1964.

Scrivin, Michael, "A Study of Radical Behaviorism," *Minnesota Studies in the Philosophy of Science,* Vol. I, *The Foundations of Science and the Concepts of Psychology,* Herbert Feigl and Michael Scrivin, eds. Minneapolis: University of Minnesota Press, 1956.

Skinner, B. F., *The Behavior of Organisms.* New York: Appleton-Century-Crofts, Inc., 1938.

———— "Behaviorism at Fifty," *Behaviorism and Phenomenology*, T. W. Wann, ed. Chicago: The University of Chicago Press, 1964.

———— "A Case History in Scientific Method," *Psychology: A Study of a Science*, S. Koch, ed. New York: McGraw Hill Company, 1959.

———— *Science and Human Behavior.* New York: The Free Press, 1953.

Wolman, Benjamin B., "Toward a Science of Psychological Science," *Scientific Psychology*, Benjamin B. Wolman, ed. New York: Basic Books, Inc., 1965.

Periodicals

Krech, David. "Psychoneurobiochemeducation." *Phi Delta Kappan*, Vol. 50, No. 7, March, 1969.

Skinner, B. F. "Are Theories of Learning Necessary?" *Psychological Review*, Vol. 57, No. 4, July, 1950.

Smart, J. J. C. "Sensations and Brain Processes." *The Philosophical Review*, Vol. LXVIII, No. 2, 1959.

Cognitive Teaching, the Field Theory, and the Functional Concept of Mind

THE COGNITIVE VIEW OF TEACHING

Today there are many disparate views of teaching based on a wide variety of psychological and philosophical foundations. Among them is a group of viewpoints which, in spite of their minor differences, share a common premise that such mental processes as understanding, insight, reflective thinking, problem solving, and self-discovery are central to teaching and learning. In this chapter we shall characterize such concepts of teaching as being *cognitive* in nature. Accordingly, the expression "cognitive view of teaching" does not represent a single theory of teaching, but refers to any notion of teaching which focuses its concern primarily on the cognitive processes we have just mentioned.

Reflective Thinking

In a democratic society we implicitly or explicitly hold the belief that every man should be treated as an end in himself and that every man is capable of deciding what is good for him as well as the best means of attaining it. This implies that, at least in principle, each individual is capable of making sound judgments if given opportunity and proper education. Hence, a member of a democratic society does not only have the right to exercise his freedom, but he also has the right to receive the kind of education which will train and develop the intellectual powers and perspective in order to be able to exercise this freedom well. As Neil Postman and Charles Weingartner, the authors of *Teaching as a Subversive Activity,* point out, our schools as instruments of a free society "must serve as the principal medium for developing in youth the attitude and skills of social, political and cultural criticism."[1] Consequently, reflective thinking must be an educational aim, because

> thinking enables us to direct our activities with foresight and to plan according to ends-in-view, or purposes of which we are aware. It enables us to act in deliberate and intentional fashion to attain future objects or to come into command of what is now distant and lacking. By putting the consequences of different ways and lines of action before the mind, it enables us to know what we are about when we act. *It converts action that is merely appetitive, blind, and impulsive into intelligent action.*[2]

In this way reflective thinking gives us a better control of our present life as well as of future possibilities. In other words, it enables us to have a rational and intelligent life by freeing us from fear, superstition, appetite and routine. It also enriches our life by giving additional meanings to things that surround us, for to a reflective thinker physical events and things are more than mere objects of perception, because they are seen as means of achieving various purposes. Objects and events appear to have different meanings after we have acquired knowledge about them, for example, a rock would have a more enriched and expanded meaning for a geologist than for a man in the street who has no geological training. But what is the nature of reflective thinking, which is said to be essential to a rational, intelligent, and free life?

The Nature of Reflective Thinking

The kind of thinking which gives us better control of our life and adds enriched meanings to our experience is more

1. Neil Postman and Charles Weingartner, *Teaching as a Subversive Activity*, p. 2.
2. John Dewey, *How We Think*, p. 17.

than a matter of entertaining ideas, recalling facts, or meandering through fantasies, for reflective thinking has a purpose, a conclusion that can be validated. In such a process our thoughts become related to each other as well as to the consequences they are likely to produce. In other words, it is a persistent and careful examination of beliefs and knowledge in relation to the evidences which support them and the consequences which are likely to follow. Reflective thinking is, then, a method of inquiry. That is, a means of resolving a conflict, a puzzle, or a problem. Consequently, it does not occur automatically or reflexively. We begin to reflect when we decide to face the difficulty and to do something about it. Or as the American philosopher Charles Peirce once said, it is the irritation of doubt which initiates genuine thinking. Once we begin to think reflectively about the encountered difficulty, we observe and relate the problem to available facts and our previous experiences to clarify the nature of the perplexity. Through this process we become aware of the obstacles as well as the resources and may even formulate possible solutions to the problem. These possible solutions are like scientific hypotheses in that they need to be tested and validated. But since not all suggested solutions can actually be tried in real situations, many of them would have to be tested covertly in our mind. That is, we need to perform mental experimentation. The final solution of the problem should be determined on the basis of this experimentation and such other confirming evidence as other people's experiences and opinions.

According to Dewey, reflective thinking has five main phases. In his words, they are:

(1) Suggestions, in which the mind leaps forward to a possible solution; (2) an intellectualization of the difficulty or perplexity that has been *felt* (directly experienced) into a *problem* to be solved, a question for which the answer must be sought; (3) the use of one suggestion after another as a leading idea, or *hypothesis*, to initiate and guide observation and other operations in collection of factual material; (4) the mental elaborations of the

idea or supposition as an idea or supposition (reasoning, in the sense in which reasoning is a part, not the whole, of inference); and (5) testing the hypothesis by overt or imaginative action.[3]

Although these five aspects of reflective thinking give us a logical and schematic description of the reflective process, they should not be understood as fixed steps to be followed; rather, they indicate the indispensable traits of reflective thinking. These phases are not rules of thinking to be obeyed, for in actual practice two or more of the phases may be passed over hastily. For example, we may formulate suggestions or hypotheses before the problem is analyzed thoroughly. In such a situation the suggestions may influence our further observation. Hence, no rules can be specifically prescribed for reflective inquiry, because the way in which these phases are managed "depends upon the intellectual tact and sensitiveness of the individual."[4] But whether we follow the five steps in the order in which they are given, or telescope some of them, the problem and its proposed solutions should always be considered in relation to past experiences, present conditions, and future possibilities. In other words, attainment of a goal or solution of a problem should always be regarded as a means for achieving future objectives. What makes reflective thinking so important is that our ability to think reflectively is believed to make us progressively more capable of handling problems of all sorts.

As was pointed out earlier, reflective thinking does not occur automatically. It is a deliberate undertaking in that thinking does not occur until we consciously decide to do something about a problem. In such an intentional and purposive affair the person's attitude is as important as the information he possesses. Unless we have the desire and the willingness to think reflectively neither our knowledge of the rules of correct thinking nor exercises in logic will make us become reflective and critical thinkers. Thus, in teaching

3. *Ibid.*, p. 107.
4. *Ibid.*, p. 116.

children to think reflectively we must not only impart rules of logic but also cultivate those attitudes which are favorable for the development of the child's ability to think. Dewey lists these attitudes as (1) open-mindedness, (2) wholeheartedness, and (3) responsibility.[5]

The attitude of open-mindeness frees us from prejudice, which prevents us from considering new problems and ideas, and different modes of thinking and acting. Open-mindedness signifies the willingness to examine the grounds of our beliefs as well as those of others. This open attitude comes from an alert curiosity, the desire to know about all possible sides of an issue, and also the recognition that even our own cherished beliefs may be wrong. An open-minded person is someone who understands the limitations of man's intelligence and the fallibility of human knowledge. The attitude of wholehearted-ness refers to the kind of enthusiasm which makes a person become completely immersed in a cause or a task. This attitude is important in moral and practical spheres as much as in the intellectual dimension of a person's life. Anyone who has divided interest and loyalty and pays only superficial attention to thinking cannot become an effective and critical thinker. It is only when a person is thoroughly interested in his subject that "questions occur to him spontaneously; a flood of suggestions pour in on him; further inquiries and readings are indicated and followed; instead of having to use his energy to hold his mind to the subject . . . the material holds and buoys his mind up and gives an onward impetus of thinking."[6] Lastly, an intellectually responsible person is someone who is willing to accept the consequences of his beliefs. Intellectual responsibility gives the person integrity, because his actions are consistent with his commitments. When children are forced to study materials which are beyond their experience and understanding they become intellectually irresponsible, because their curiosity is not stimulated. That is, they become indifferent to the meanings and the possible consequences of

5. *Ibid.*, pp. 30–33.
6. *Ibid.*, pp. 31–32.

what they learn on their thought and conduct. As Dewey reminds us, in teaching children to become effective thinkers there should not be any separation between knowledge of logic and of qualities of character, rather they need to be integrated with each other.

Cognitive Teaching and Reflective Thinking

From the cognitive standpoint teaching is a means by which the learner is helped and guided in developing his ability to solve problems, or to think reflectively about whatever he is studying. Cognitive teaching, which is synonymous with reflective teaching, is problem-centered and hence it is more interested in engaging students in "those activities which produce knowledge: defining, questioning, observing, classifying, generalizing, verifying, applying."[7] Accordingly, the primary aim in teaching a subject is not to transmit a store of knowledge to the learner but it is to get the students to think as historians, biologists, sociologists, and philosophers do about their subjects, and to have them become capable of controlling their own activities and correcting their own mistakes. In this kind of teaching "the focus of intellectual energy becomes the active investigation of structure and relationships, rather than the passive reception of someone else's story."[8] However, this does not mean that facts are unnecessary, but it does imply that acquired facts receive their meaning as they are related to the solution of a particular problem or achieving a specific objective. Thus any knowledge or information unrelated to the learner's attempt to solve a problem is useless.[9] On the other hand, if cognitive or reflective teaching is successful students will become self-reliant, self-confident, and effective problem solvers. In contrast to the so-called expository teaching in which the teacher

---

7. Postman, *Teaching as Subversive Activity*, p. 36.
8. *Ibid.*, p. 29.
9. Jerome S. Bruner, *Toward A Theory of Instruction*, p. 53.

predetermines the nature and content of learning experiences as well as the mode and style of exposition, reflective teaching regards the student as a sort of "co-author" of the method and content of instruction. In such a teaching-learning situation the learner is no longer a passive listener, but he is an inquirer who is aware of alternative courses of action, their possible consequences, and the possibility of error in his judgment as well. The teacher too must become an active inquirer who is interested in having his students ask questions about the meaning and the structure of new and old ideas. He must also treat the initial answer given by the student as the starting point of "a process in which both teacher and student give themselves to the task of engaging in communication in order to gain and share understanding."[10] In order to prevent children from becoming discouraged and withdrawing from reflective thinking the teacher must give students the assurance that they will not be punished for disagreeing or making mistakes. In a similar vein, Martin Buber, a Jewish philosopher, pointed out that unless there is *mutuality* in teacher-pupil relationships even a small problem becomes a major issue and the "oppositeness" between the teacher and his students becomes a battle of will. By the term *mutuality* Buber meant the kind of trust or confidence which convinces the student that the teacher is there for him and that he will not be used as a means for some other purpose. Without this kind of trust and assurance the teacher's criticisms and probing questions are likely to squelch the student's desire to think, to express his ideas freely, and to participate actively in the process of inquiry. In effective teaching, then, the nature of teacher-pupil relationships is as vital as the method and content of instruction and the environmental climate of the teaching-learning situation, because "the beliefs, feelings, and assumptions of teachers are the air of a learning environment; they determine the quality of life within it."[11] "A teacher who

10. Gordon H. Hullfish and Philip G. Smith, *Reflective Thinking*, p. 197.
11. Postman, *Teaching as a Subversive Activity*, p. 33.

views himself as a "pleasant collaborator" in a thoughtful experience will dismiss no answers arbitrarily, nor accept any perfunctorily. He will be sure, insofar as the complexity of the human relationship permits, that *a quality of trust* pervades his relationship with students."[12]

Postman and Weingartner point out that a reflective teacher rarely tells his students what they should think and know, for he is more interested in asking questions and engaging the learner's mind to unsuspected possibilities. Consequently, such a teacher does not accept a single statement as an answer to a question. As an inquirer himself he encourages student-student discussions rather than student-teacher interaction. The reflective teacher usually prepares his materials based on the responses given by his students rather than follow some predetermined structure of a discipline. Hence, his lesson plans are problems to be solved by his students. As a result of cognitive (reflective) teaching children become competent in coping with problems and efficient in future learning. This type of teaching also makes it possible for the learner to discover for himself the basic principles, concepts, and structure of what he is studying. In self-discovery new insights are obtained by rearranging and reinterpreting what is already known. Certainly new information and evidence are helpful, but self-discovery does not depend upon them. What is the method of self-discovery, and how can it be taught to children?

Bruner on Learning by Discovery

One contemporary psychologist who has attempted to relate his study of such cognitive processes as perception, memory, thinking, and learning to teaching is Jerome S. Bruner, co-director of the Center for Cognitive Studies at Harvard University. In recent years many educational psychologists, curriculum specialists, and teachers have been

---

12. Hullfish, *Reflective Thinking*, p. 203.

influenced by Bruner's view of learning by discovery, teaching theories, and the role of the structure of knowledge in learning. Consequently, an examination of these views will be profitable for us.

According to Bruner, the working heuristics of discovery can be learned only by actually trying to solve problems oneself. To put it differently, the more one tries to work out solutions to problems and figure out things for himself, the more one gains new insights. Thus, only by engaging in inquiry can we improve the art and the technique of problem solving and self-discovery. For Bruner, learning by discovery has a number of beneficial effects: it increases intellectual potency, it causes the learner to value intrinsic rather than extrinsic rewards, and it aids in conserving memory.[13] In other words, by emphasizing discovery the child learns to organize his experiences in such a way as to discover regularity and relatedness, and also to distinguish relevant evidence from irrelevant facts. Furthermore, he learns a variety of ways of solving problems and also becomes progressively more effective and efficient in what he does. Secondly, children often learn knowledge or skills as a result of rewards coming from outside, i.e., extrinsic rewards, and more often than not, children who behave for extrinsic rewards are likely to conform to what is expected of them. They become primarily "outer-directed" men. Bruner hypothesizes that approaching learning as *discovering something* rather than as learning about something will lead a child to act in terms of self-reward, intrinsic reward, that is, to be rewarded by discovery itself. Learning for intrinsic reward eventually frees the child from immediate stimulus control and he becomes competence-oriented so that he can be more of an "inner-directed man." Lastly, concerning the effect of learning by discovery on the conservation of memory, since human beings seem to be able to store more information than they can spontaneously recall, the main problem in human memory

13. Jerome S. Bruner, *On Knowing*, pp. 87–90, 92, 94–95.

is that of effective retrieval. Bruner is convinced that the key to retrieval is organization of information. He contends that there is sufficient evidence to support the assertion that, in general, any information organized around the interests and the cognitive structure of the learner can be most efficiently recalled. Hence, the only means by which we can reduce the quick rate of loss of human memory is to organize facts according to the basic principles and concepts from which they were inferred. Further, "the very attitude and activities that characterize figuring out or discovering things for oneself also seem to have the effect of conserving memory."[14] In addition to these effects, the learning experiences resulting from self-discovery give us an increased awareness of the connections and continuities between what we learn and what we do. As a result, we are likely to see our activities in a broader context and thus gain more control of our acts in relation to an end in view. As Hullfish and Smith remarked, "learning, the construction of experience, is always a matter of fitting and refitting into a meaningful whole that which is known and that which seems likely but which must remain uncertain until all of the pieces are brought together."[15] In learning by discovery knowledge already possessed by the learner is used to gain new insights, and in the process old knowledge itself becomes reconstructed.

Before we move on to consider Bruner's cognitive theory of teaching a few words must be said about his view of the role of intuitive thinking in problem solving and learning by discovery. Intuitive thinking, according to Bruner, is a process of arriving at tentative solutions to a problem without going through analytic thinking, which involves well-defined steps, explicit criteria, and evidence in validating proposed solutions. Analytic thinking is at the core of reflective thinking or problem solving, and it often involves deductive reasoning and a step-by-step process of induction and experimentation. In contrast to the analytic approach to inquiry, intuitive

14. Jerome S. Bruner, *The Process of Education*, p. 96.
15. Hullfish, *Reflective Thinking*, p. 206.

thinking does not depend on explicit steps or procedures. But the thinker arrives or leaps at an answer without being aware of the supporting reasons and evidence. Only after a careful examination can he say whether the proposed solution is sound or not. In a sense, intuitive thinking is a shortcut to new hypotheses and informed hunches to be tested, and as such, it is economical in both time and effort in dealing with an indeterminate state. A precondition for one's ability to think intuitively is familiarity with the domain of knowledge involved, however, so before encouraging students to think intuitively we must have them become thoroughly acquainted with the subject. It is also important that the teacher be able to distinguish careless mistakes from those honest errors resulting from intuitive leaps, particularly because the students who feel insecure and lack self-confidence are often unwilling to risk making even honest mistakes for fear of disapproval and rejection.

A Theory of Teaching

Much of our discussion thus far has been centered on the nature and effect of reflective thinking on learning. We have not said much about a theory of cognitive or reflective teaching, mainly because no one has yet constructed such a theory. However, Bruner regards a sound theory of teaching as essential in guiding us toward achieving certain instructional objectives. The elements he sees as necessary to a theory of teaching are: (1) predisposition toward learning, (2) structure of knowledge, (3) optimal sequence, and (4) reward and punishment.[16]

The first element is concerned with specifying the conditions which predispose a child to learn effectively. Bruner points out that the teaching-learning situation is a dynamic process in which two or more individuals are involved. Hence, if a child is to cope with school and engage in learning

16. Bruner, *A Theory of Instruction*, pp. 40–42.

he must have minimal mastery of social skills in order to maintain many different kinds of relationships with others. Among other important factors such as cultural background, social class, and sex the way in which the child explores different alternative courses of action directly affects his learning and problem solving. Bruner names three different approaches to the regulation of the child's exploratory or search behavior: activation, maintenance, and direction. Or to put it another way, "exploration of alternatives requires something to get started, something to keep it going, and something to keep it from being random."[17] This means the learning situation must be such that the child's curiosity is aroused enough to activate his exploratory behavior. Once the search behavior has begun it is important that the benefit from such exploration be greater than the risk involved. Learning in the presence of a teacher should minimize the risks and make the consequences of errors less painful if the teacher guides the child's activities and also shows him the causes of failure. But in order to make the direction of the exploratory behavior appropriate it is necessary that the child have a clear understanding of the goal and knowledge of the relevant means which will be helpful in attaining it. Moreover, in encouraging children to explore alternatives we must not only cultivate the attitude of healthy skepticism toward old cherished beliefs, "sacred cows," and established doctrines which have been taken for granted but we must also convince the child that reflective thinking and the use of his mind are important. That is, the child's own belief that men can effectively deal with his problems and perplexities by the use of his mind is an essential factor in activating him to explore alternatives.

In clarifying the concept of the structure of knowledge, Bruner asserts that, "any idea or problem or body of knowledge can be presented in a form simple enough so that any particular learner can understand it in a recognizable form."[18]

17. *Ibid.*, p. 43.
18. *Ibid.*, p. 44.

This is, of course, an extension of a theorem in A. M. Turing's theory of computation, which contends that any problem that can be solved can be solved by simpler means. In other words, in Bruner's view any complex problem can be analyzed into a set of simpler elements which can then be dealt with in simpler and more elementary operations. Therefore, knowledge about anything can be divided into simpler units for children to grasp. Hence, the structure and the form of knowledge become an indispensable element in Bruner's theory of teaching.

For Bruner, knowledge about anything can be represented enactively, iconically, and symbolically.[19] Enactive representation of knowledge refers to knowing by doing. For example, we learn how to type, to swim, or to ride a bicycle by performing certain activities. By doing these activities we gain knowledge of things appropriate to achieving certain results, but we speak of our doing this or that without being able to explain the principles involved. When we represent some segment of knowledge with the help of mental images we are using iconic representation. The images are not exact duplicates of nature; they represent only general pictures of nature. For instance, we may not be able to give an exhaustive mathematical definition of a trapezoid, but we may be able to represent it as a plane figure with four sides, two of which are parallel. The symbolic representation of knowledge involves using words or mathematical symbols. It has to do with "putting things into a symbol system with rules for manipulating, for decomposing and recomposing and transforming and turning symbols on their heads that makes it possible to explore things not present, not pictorial, and indeed not in existence."[20] This is the most abstract way of representing knowledge; therefore, children, or those who are at the beginning level of a subject, may find it difficult to use. Bruner correctly points out that some forms of knowledge can be

19. *Ibid.,* pp. 44–48.
20. Jerome S. Bruner, "Needed: A Theory of Instruction," *Contemporary Thought on Teaching.* Ronald T. Hyman, ed., p. 158.

more readily represented enactively or iconically, while other forms are more conveniently represented symbolically. Bruner goes on to say that actions (enactive representation), pictures (iconic representation), and symbols (symbolic representation) would have varying degrees of difficulty and usefulness for people of different ages and different intellectual, social, and cultural backgrounds. But as Bruner reminds us, we should not create a structure of knowledge by beginning with the most abstract symbolic representation. On the contrary, we must begin with enactive and iconic representations (actions and pictures) not only because our intellectual development goes from enactive to iconic to symbolic representations but also because the meaningful understanding of the symbolic system is possible only if we relate it to what we do and the mental images we already have.

In addition to these three modes of representation, Bruner characterizes knowledge by its economy and power. *Economy* refers to the amount of knowledge one has to have in order to comprehend a particular domain of knowledge. The more information one has to have to understand something or to deal with a problem, the more steps one has to take to accomplish the task, and the more things one has to know or to do, the less the economy. Knowledge can be organized in certain characteristic ways to increase the economy of a particular domain of knowledge. For example, items of information can be organized alphabetically or diagrammatic notations can be used to represent certain concepts or operations (e.g., geometric theorems, operant conditioning, etc.). (Economy, which varies with the mode of representation, is also a function of the sequence in which knowledge is learned or presented; see the discussion of optimal sequencing below.) As for power, the effective *power* of any particular way of structuring a domain of knowledge for a particular learner refers to the generative value of his set of learned propositions."[21] In other words, the power of a particular way of

21. Bruner, *A Theory of Instruction*, p. 47.

organizing knowledge to facilitate effective learning depends upon the capability of the structure of knowledge to generate new hypotheses and explanations. In principle, economy and power are independent, so the most powerful explanations may not necessarily be the most economical or the simplest. In consonance with an assumption underlying the principle of parsimony ("Occam's razor"), that nature is simple, the most powerful structuring of knowledge is usually the most economical.

Returning to the elements in Bruner's theory of teaching, the third element, optimal sequencing, is important because teaching is a matter of guiding the learner through a series of topics and problems according to the sequence most appropriate for the learner to grasp effectively what he is learning. Consequently, the nature of the sequence adopted determines how effectively and how easily the learner will achieve mastery of a subject. Bruner rightly points out that there is no single sequence which is appropriate for all learners, for the optimum in any particular situation depends upon the learner's past training, his stage of development, his socio-cultural backgrounds, the nature of the material, and such variables as speed of learning, mode of representation, economy, and power. However, since our intellectual development goes from enactive to iconic to symbolic representations, the optimum sequence in any subject is likely to follow the same pattern. This implies that the best sequencing begins with the presentation of materials which are familiar to the learner's sensory experiences and activities and then eventually moves to more abstract materials. Accordingly, Bruner suggests that we might first give the child many particular instances so that he can grasp the underlying regularity, which can be made clearer by then giving him many contrasting cases. We should avoid having the child symbolize prematurely; he should not be asked to repeat words and concepts until their meanings are understood either by manipulation or in images. Lastly, we should encourage the child to plod and leap. That is, let him approach a particular problem by small steps, but also permit him to take leaps and big guesses, because we often become aware of what we know by guessing.

Rewards and punishments are important in learning, for they are often the child's means of knowing about the results of his activities in seeking a goal. Therefore, teaching should be carried on in such a way that the learner can receive corrective information at the most appropriate time and place. But in effective learning it is essential that the child become an independent problem solver who rewards and punishes himself on the basis of the adequacy of his effort. By emphasizing rewards and punishments from an outside agent we often make the child think that the agents of reward and punishment are the major initiating force for learning rather than his own success or failure. In brief, the learner should be made to regard problem solving and discovery as intrinsic rewards for learning.

Some Comments on Bruner's Concept of the Structure of Knowledge and His Theory of Teaching

A few words need to be said about Bruner's concept of the structure of knowledge before we move on to evaluate Lewin's field theory. On the basis of what Bruner has written about the structure of knowledge, it is not always clear what he means by the term *structure*. Sometimes he speaks of it as something inherent in all disciplines. In this sense teaching the structure of a discipline means helping students to discover what is already in the discipline. At other times he talks as if we can impose a structure upon knowledge. Hence, structure in this sense is not thought of as that which is inherent in the nature of the discipline but as a way in which various experts organize their fields according to differing rationale and criteria. There may, therefore, be more than one structure to a discipline. Pedagogically, it is more useful to think of the structure of knowledge as consisting of certain basic concepts and principles around which the specific content of a discipline is organized. The arrangement of these concepts and principles—or organizers, as Ausubel calls them—can be altered to suit the learner's interest, background, maturity, and rate of growth.

Bruner's view that any subject matter can be presented in a form simple enough so that any learner can understand it requires further clarification. If he means that understanding necessarily follows from any simple presentation, because it is used as a defining characteristic of "simple presentation," Bruner is doing nothing more than making a tautological statement, which is always true by definition. That is, if simple presentation and understanding a discipline are necessarily connected to each other by definition, then what Bruner asserts is no longer an empirical principle but only a form of redundant statement. However, if Bruner is suggesting that there are specific modes of presentation which he regards as simple, then it is possible that a child might not understand the material even though it was presented in a simple enough form. In any event, understanding presupposes a certain amount of previous knowledge and experience in many disciplines and therefore it may not be possible in every case to present certain ideas and principles to a child so that he can understand the discipline in a recognizable form. For example, in what simple ways could we explain the difficulties of two-sided interactionism or the principle of conservation of energy to a grade school child? As to Bruner's suggested theory of instruction, its four elements, predisposition, structuring of knowledge, sequencing, and reward and punishment, are an attempt to explain certain major variables which affect the teaching-learning process. Yet, there are other crucial factors which have not been sufficiently explained. For instance, in any teaching-learning situation the cognitive and affective growth of the learner is as important as the socio-cultural climate of the school and the classroom as social systems. But these variables play very little role in Bruner's scheme. And certainly the nature of interpersonal relationships among children, and teachers' personality traits and their relationship to certain pedagogical strategies cannot be ignored in an adequate theory of teaching. Admittedly, construction of a theory of this type is extremely complex and difficult. But if we are to make teaching more than a craft, much more empirical and theoretical work needs to be done about the teaching process in relation to these variables.

In summary, the cognitive theory of teaching is based on the premise that worthwhile and productive learning occurs most effectively only within the context of genuine inquiry resulting from the learner's recognition of certain perplexities and his willingness to do something about them. If successful, cognitive or reflective teaching will help the student become increasingly competent in handling problems and maintaining all sorts of relationships with others. It is a process in which the teacher and the student are actively involved in an intelligent action directed by goals. Therefore, meaningful learning experiences are the result of the teacher's guidance as much as of what the learner can do on his own. As Dewey put it:

> When the parent or teacher has provided the conditions which stimulate thinking and has taken a sympathetic attitude toward the activities of the learner by entering into a common or conjoint experience, all has been done which a second party can do to instigate learning. The rest lies with the one directly concerned. If he cannot devise his own way out he will not learn, not even if he can recite some correct answers with one hundred per cent accuracy. . . . This does not mean that the teacher is to stand off and look on; the alternative to furnishing ready-made subject matter and listening to the accuracy with which it is reproduced is not quiescence, but participation, sharing, in an activity. In such shared activity, the teacher is a learner, and the learner is, without knowing it, a teacher and upon the whole, the less consciousness there is, on either side, of either giving or receiving instruction, the better.[22]

22. John Dewey, *Democracy and Education*, p. 188.

THE FIELD THEORY OF BEHAVIOR

Of the psychological theories of human behavior and learning, Kurt Lewin's (1890–1947) field theory is perhaps most consistent with the cognitive view of teaching we have just discussed. In a very real sense, cognitive teaching can be seen as an application of Lewin's theory of behavior to teaching. As we discuss the basic tenets of the field theory its connection with cognitive teaching will become more apparent.

Unlike Skinner, Lewin did not regard the proper function of psychology as the formulation of a purely descriptive and classificatory account of human behavior. On the contrary, he argued that we should study human behavior (B) as a function (f) of the person's (P) total environment (E). Lewin's concept of behavior is then explained in the formula $B=f(P.E.)$. What is necessary is to develop constructs and methods which can account for the forces underlying man's behavior. From this perspective, the general laws of psychology are statements about the relationship between the constructs. And since the person is always at the center of behaving and acting "the [psychological] field which influences an individual should be described not in 'objective physicalistic' terms, but in the way in which it exists for that person at that time."[23] Thus the teacher cannot give helpful guidance to his pupil if he cannot "see" the psychological world in which the child lives.

> To describe a situation "objectively" in psychology actually means to describe the situation as a totality of those facts and of only those facts which make up the field of that individual. To substitute for that world of the individual with the world of the teacher, of the physicist, or of anybody else is to be, not objective, but wrong.[24]

This suggests that psychology must find those scientific constructs which can adequately represent the psychological

23. Kurt Lewin, *Field Theory in Social Science*, Dorwing Cartwright, ed., p. 62.
24. *Ibid.*

factors and their relatedness in such a way that the behavior of the individual can be explained and predicted. It also means that the elements within a person's psychological world cannot be studied apart from the situation as a whole, for human behavior, as Lewin sees it, is the function of the person and the total environmental situation. Thus, a person's own perception of his world is an indispensable variable affecting his behavior. The advocates of cognitive teaching insist that our knowledge of the learner's own perception of his environment is vital to effective teaching and learning. From Lewin's standpoint, our preoccupation with specific observable responses can give us only an inadequate and partial explanation of human behavior.

In an attempt to devise a theoretical framework for representing environmental variables as they impinge upon the psychological person, Lewin utilized many topological concepts. Geometric concepts, which deal with transformations in space, such as *inside, outside, next to,* as well as *vector, valance, equilibrium,* etc., which have been borrowed from physics and chemistry, are used to describe the psychological motions of a person in his psychological environment. The use of topological terms is particularly appropriate because Lewin was concerned with psychological field, that is, the total psychological world in which a person lives. What makes the field theory so distinct from other perspectives is that analysis of behavior does not begin with a separate consideration of the specific elements within a situation. A field theorist begins with a study of the situation as a whole, then he analyzes its various parts more specifically. This approach to the study of human behavior is consistent with the premise that human behavior cannot be adequately understood apart from man's psychological environment.

Life Space

Life space, a key concept in Lewin's theory, refers to the person's psychological environment (field) as it exists for him.

It is the contemporary psychological world of a person and "at any given time it includes all facts that have existence and excludes those that do not have existence *for the individual or group under study*."[25] Life space includes everything of which a person is aware. His goals, his memories, his anticipations, things he wants to avoid, the barriers which impede his action, and the resources which may be of help to his effort. Even if the things in the life space of a person do not happen to be objectively true, they are likely to affect the person's behavior as long as they are psychological facts to him. The properties of the life space are dependent upon the person's psychological, social, and emotional history. Thus behavior is determined by the condition of the life space at the time behavior occurs. The structure of our life space undergoes changes as new learning experiences accrue and the altered conditions of the life space in turn influence our behavior. As was indicated earlier, life space contains only those things of which the person is conscious. There are other variables outside of the person's psychological world which may still affect his behavior. The items which are not within the life space are included in what Lewin refers to as the *foreign hull,* which surrounds the life space. And though what was in the foreign hull can be incorporated into life space later, the foreign hull itself is not a part of life space.

Valance and Vector

We live and move in the psychological world of the life space according to certain pulls and pushes coming from its various regions, which contain goals. If a goal in a region pulls the person toward it, it is said to have positive valance. But if a region pushes a person away, or if he avoids it, it is said to have negative valance. When a life space has more than one region with positive or negative valances, the person is said to

25. *Ibid.*, p. xi.

have a conflict. For example, he may be attracted by a favorite program on TV and he may be pulled toward a long awaited movie being shown at a nearby theatre. In a situation of this sort, the person is more likely to move toward the region which has the greater positive valance. In the case of negative valance, the person moves away from the region which has the greater negative valance.

In addition to the concept of valance, Lewin introduced the term *vector* to indicate the path the individual is most likely to take. Vectors in a life space represent forces of varying magnitudes operating in different directions. In Lewin's system arrows were used to indicate the direction of the force and the length of the arrow represented the strength of the force. Hence, our knowledge of another person's life space and the valances therein will tell us about the alternative courses of action that are possible for him. A further analysis of vectors in the life space will enable us to determine the course of action he is most likely to take. For instance, accurate information about the child's psychological position in relation to his goals and the ways in which the child relates to groups, his peers, ideas, and physical surroundings will make it possible to predict what he is likely to do in a certain situation. Of course, the more information we have about the psychological forces impinging upon the individual the more accurate our prediction will become.

Need

In explaining the motivating variables responsible for initiating behavior, Lewin uses the term *need* to represent a motivated state. That is, when a need is aroused a state of disequilibrium is brought about. Disequilibrium or a state of unequal tension sets off the psychological motion to restore equilibrium, thereby satisfying one's need. Hence, as the advocates of cognitive teaching contend, genuine reflective thinking cannot occur unless the learner himself recognizes the disequilibrium and decides to do something about it rather than ignoring it or escaping from it. Hence, Lewin's account of the ways in which a person decides to act in a particular way is *in principle* similar to the view held by the advocates of cognitive teaching, that genuine reflective thinking cannot occur unless the learner himself recognizes the disequilibrium and chooses to do something about it.

Learning as a Change in Cognitive Structure

To Lewin, learning involved at least four different categories of change: (1) changes in cognitive structure, (2) changes in motivation, (3) changes in group belongingness or ideology, and (4) changes in the voluntary control of the body musculature.[26] However, Lewin pointed out that changes in the likes or dislikes of a person (category 2), breaking away from the standards of one group to another and changes in beliefs (category 3), and the development of skills (category 4) all involve changes in cognitive structure, i.e., the way in which a person sees his psychological world. For our purpose here, interpreting Lewin's concept of learning as a change in cognitive structure is adequate.

Before any learning occurs a problematic situation represents an undifferentiated region of life space. In any indeterminate situation we do not have a clear idea about the ends-means connection, so we do not know what we must do to achieve an objective. But as a result of learning experience unstructured life space of the person is changed by differentiation, generalization, and restructuring. *Differentiation* is the subdivision of unstructured regions of a life space into smaller regions and awareness of the specific aspects of these regions. *Generalization* is a process by which various regions of life space are categorized according to certain common elements found therein, so that regions, subregions, and their elements

26. *Ibid.*, p. 66.

can be identified as a class of objects, events, or ideas. Thus a teacher may formulate a generalized concept of teaching and learning based on specific instances of teaching and learning. *Restructuring* of life space means changing the direction of movements in one's life space by relating the regions in a way different from their earlier connection by giving different meaning and significance to them. Lewin's example of a man moving into a new town illustrates the concept of learning as a change in cognitive structure. A man arrives at the depot of a new town as a stranger. Though he has already rented an apartment and he knows his address, he does not know how to get there, because he forgot to bring a map of the town. As figure 1 shows,[27] the person (P) is in the station (ST). The region between the person in the station and his apartment (A) is undifferentiated (U), because he does not know anything about the route to the apartment, the area surrounding the apartment, or how far it is between the apartment and the

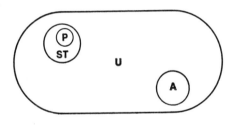

FIG. 1

station. The stranger makes some inquiries and learns that streetcar D will take him directly to the apartment. Now the previously undifferentiated region between the station and the apartment is somewhat differentiated by his knowledge of

27. *Ibid.*, pp. 70–71 for figures 1, 2, and 3.

streetcar D. This is shown in figure 2. As the man finds his way
to work (W) and around the town he gains more information
about the routes between the station, apartment,

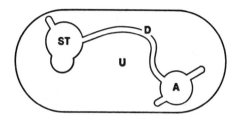

FIG. 2

and his office. As shown in figure 3 this region of the man's life
space has become highly differentiated. A similar process

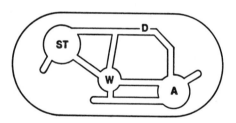

FIG. 3

of differentiation occurs in his social life as well. But since all
learning does not necessarily entail differentiation of a previously unstructured region, we may only need to increase the
vector magnitude. That is, we may change the intensity or
speed of our psychological motions. For example, the
stranger in the story may find it necessary to travel faster
and/or oftener, or slower and less often, etc., without changing his routes at all.

Though Lewin did not say much about the pedagogical ramifications of his theory, there is little doubt that the cognitive view of teaching and the field theory of learning are based on the same premise that human behavior, which is purposive and goal directed, is the result of a simultaneous and mutual stimulation between the person and his total environment. In other words, man's deliberate behavior is an outcome of a transactional process in which the environment affects the person's way of looking at his world and the person "does" something to his world because he sees it as having this or that meaning and significance. Even when behavior is activated by a state of need and disequilibrium, genuine reflection and learning cannot be initiated unless the learner becomes conscious of the problem (irritation of doubt) and decides to do something about it. Hence, learning occurs most effectively when the learner is involved in a reflective inquiry. Furthermore, Lewin's assertion that learning results in a reconstruction of the child's experience is an extension of the view that learning and a change in cognitive structure are synonymous. Certainly the elements in reflective thinking are essential ingredients in the process of differentiating, generalizing, and restructuring regions of life space. In short, the cognitive view of teaching is an application of the field theory of behavior to teaching and they are both founded on the same philosophical conception of the mind, the study of which is central to psychology and the cultivation of which is central to teaching.

THE FUNCTIONAL CONCEPT OF MIND

To foresee a terminus of an act is to have a basis upon which to observe, to select, and to order objects and our own capacities. To do these things means to have a mind—for mind is precisely intentional purposeful activity controlled by perception of facts and their relationships to one another. To have a mind to do a thing is to foresee a future possibility; it is to have a plan for its accomplishment; it is to note the means which make the plan capable of execution and the obstructions in the way,—or if it is really a *mind* to do the thing and not a vague aspiration—it is to have a plan which takes account of resources and difficulties.[28]

These words of John Dewey succinctly explain the functional concept of mind which underlies the field theory of behavior and the cognitive view of teaching. Both of these viewpoints are based on the premise that mind is not a separate and unextended substance, a spiritual entity, exempt from the laws of nature. The term *mind* refers to the ways in which man as a total organism functions. It is a means of describing man's capacity to act intentionally and purposefully by taking into account the resources, difficulties, and possible consequences of the various courses of action available to him. Mind thus represents a quality of action rather than a thing or a special power by virtue of which we carry on our mental functions. To speak of man's mind is "to speak in a highly abbreviated way of a large class of his special abilities and capacities—to think, to engage in intentional actions, to sense, to feel, and the like."[29] George Herbert Mead (1863–1931), a leading Deweyan philosopher, expressed a similar belief that mind is neither a transcendental entity nor a mysterious spiritual power, nor even a special biological endowment. Mead argued that *mind* stands for man's functional activity of dealing with problematic situations. In other words, the human mind is the problem-solving ability, which developed as a result of man's attempt to maintain all sorts of relationships with others. And though the mind is not a unique biological endowment, it appeared because man has the kind of nervous system which makes social process possible. Mind could not have emerged without the social process. In Mead's words,

> mind, as constructive or reflective or problem-solving thinking, is the socially acquired means or mechanism or apparatus whereby

28. Dewey, *Democracy and Education*, p. 120.
29. Bruce Aune, *Knowledge, Man, and Nature*, p. 226.

the human individual solves the various problems of environmental adjustment which arise to confront him in the course of his experience, and which prevent his conduct from proceeding harmoniously on its way, until they have thus been dealt with.[30]

From the functional point of view, the key to the understanding of mind is the notion of sociality, or those social acts which involve the cooperation of more than one individual. It is because men can act cooperatively by helping and sharing things with others and also because man has been able to communicate with gestures and language that he came to possess a mind. The mind, or the self, emerges from one's ability to adopt his group's attitude and stimulate himself as he stimulates others. Thus, the term *mind* refers to the purposive and anticipatory qualities of human action, which serve as a means by which the individual adjusts himself to his environment in an increasingly effective way. The term mind should not be understood as a noun representing a thing; it should be used as an adjective, an adverb, or a verb. We can speak of "minding" and acting "mindfully." To mind something or to act mindfully is to be able to plan one's actions and to control certain aspects of one's surroundings so that what is done at any particular time is done as a means for attaining some future ends. Hence, the mind is an "ability to respond to present stimuli on the basis of anticipation of future possible consequences. But the ability to deal with problems insightfully, and to reflectively think about whatever affects one's life could not have emerged apart from communication within a social process. In other words, in his social interactions man becomes an object for himself by assuming the roles of others."[31] He not only does what various roles demand that he do but also sees himself as others see him. As sociologist Charles Cooley maintained, our concept of the self is based on our perception of the ways in which other people see us. Thus other people's actions and reactions toward us

30. George H. Mead, *Mind, Self, and Society*, p. 308.
31. George H. Mead, *The Philosophy of the Present*, pp. 184–187.

serve as a mirror in which the self is reflected. By assuming what Mead called the role of the generalized other, "We must regard mind, then, as arising and developing within the social process within the empirical matrix of social interaction."[32] It is this ability of the individual to respond to himself as others would and also to use significant symbols, gestures and speech, rather than automatic responses to external stimuli, that constitutes the mind.

The functional concept of mind can be characterized as naturalistic in that it is not based on the assumption that there are entities which transcend the natural world. From this perspective the mind as an unextended substance is meaningless, save in its metaphorical meaning, because the mind as a metaphysical entity is not knowable through empirical experiences. Moreover, if the mind can be explained within the naturalistic frame of reference (as in the functional concept), how can we justify positing a spiritual entity for which there is no good positive evidence to support its existence? In addition to being naturalistic, the functional concept of mind is also monistic in that it makes no separation between the mind and the body as two distinct entities. Of course the mental can be distinguished from the physical without implying their separate and independent existence as substances. And because the functional concept is monistic as well as naturalistic it avoids the dualistic dilemma of having to explain how two so radically different substances as mind and body can causally affect each other.

CONCLUDING COMMENTS

Today cognitive teaching is in vogue and many of its proponents regard it as the answer to most, if not all of our educational and even social and moral problems. With its emphasis on problem solving and self-discovery, cognitive

32. Mead, *Mind, Self, Society*, p. 133.

teaching is believed to be the most effective means by which our children can be educated to become emotionally stable, socially efficient, intellectually competent, and morally upright individuals. But even those who do not see cognitive or reflective teaching as a panacea often regard it as inherently superior to expository teaching, which is thought of as leading to empty and irrelevant verbalisms. In other words, the proponents of reflective teaching assume that the only knowledge worth having is the kind which comes from self-discovery through problem solving. This means they regard expository teaching as inferior to reflective teaching by its very nature. The belief that expository teaching is educationally impotent is widely held. If it is not explicitly stated by many teachers and students, the belief is clearly reflected in their disdain for more traditional teaching procedures such as lectures, recitations, exercises, and tests. Even many of those teachers and professors who conduct their classes in a conventional expository manner would insist that under ideal conditions, that is, if classes were smaller, resources more plentiful, schedules more flexible, and their teaching load lighter, they would adopt the problem solving and self-discovery approach in their classes. In other words, expository teaching is often seen as a necessary evil to be lived with until such time as ideal teaching conditions become available. But in spite of the high and sometimes exaggerated praise and endorsement, reflective teaching is not without its critics, and their criticism should not be dismissed lightly.

A CRITICISM OF LEARNING BY DISCOVERY

According to David P. Ausubel, an educational psychologist, not only has the proper function of learning by discovery or problem solving been exaggerated but its rationale has been misunderstood. He argues that problem-solving experience is not inherently meaningful nor would expository learning necessarily lead to blindly memorized, glib verbalisms. On the contrary, both problem solving and expository teaching can be either rote or meaningful depending upon the conditions under which learning takes place. Ausubel goes on to point out that "in both instances meaningful learning takes place if the learning task can be related in nonarbitrary, substantive fashion to what the learner already knows, and if the learner adopts a corresponding learning set to do so."[33] Teaching by verbal exposition becomes ineffective and meaningless if the verbal techniques are inappropriate to the age of the children, or if facts are presented without organizing or explanatory principles and concepts, if new materials are not related to knowledge already in the learner's possession, or if evaluative procedures are used which measure only ability to recall and to recognize discrete facts. Similarly, reflective teaching can be equally meaningless and rote if pupils are made to engage in a series of activities which have been prescribed by the teacher or some other expert. One of the necessary requirements in so-called discovery teaching is that problems be structured carefully and pertinent data arranged skillfully by others so that students can ultimately "discover by themselves." Without such careful planning the teaching-learning situation would simply become chaotic if children were allowed to discover new knowledge in the same way in which scholars and scientists are said to discover it because students lack the kind of knowledge, experience, skill, and even the patience of scholars and scientists. Moreover, it is doubtful that many teachers themselves have had any experience of self-discovery purely on their own. Ausubel further points out that teaching by discovery is useful primarily in teaching children who are in their concrete stage of cognitive development. That is, in general elementary school children depend on concrete experiences for understanding abstract concepts and propositions. Therefore, in learning relational concepts and unfamiliar and difficult ideas it is most helpful if children are permitted to relate their concrete experiences with the

---

33. David P. Ausubel, "Some Psychological and Educational Limitations of Learning by Discovery," *Readings in School Learning*, David P. Ausubel, ed., p. 267.

actual process of generalizing and abstracting from empirical data. However, when students have reached the abstract stage of cognitive development in which new concepts and principles are grasped directly, it is unnecessary to use concrete experiences as the primary vehicle of learning. Here it is more efficient to help students understand new concepts and information directly through proper expository teaching in which new materials are explained. Even if we grant that reflective teaching is always superior to other kinds of teaching, the notion that every child must discover every bit of knowledge for and by himself is contrary to the very concept of culture, because, as Ausubel says,

> perhaps the most unique attribute of human culture, which distinguishes it from every other kind of social organization in the animal kingdom, is precisely the fact that accumulated discoveries of millennia can be transmitted to each succeeding generation in the course of childhood and youth, and need not be discovered anew by each generation. This miracle of culture is made possible only because it is so much less time-consuming to communicate and explain an idea meaningfully to others than to require them to re-discover it by themselves.[34]

In discussing the means by which the heuristics of discovery can be taught to children, Bruner suggested that the only way of accomplishing this is to have children participate in problem solving and thinking reflectively. But Ausubel points out that there is no transfer of learning from mental exercises to growth in general intellectual competence: "Critical thinking ability can only be enhanced within a context of a specific discipline. Grand strategies of discovery do not seem to be transferable across disciplinary lines."[35] Even if we agree that children's problem-solving and critical-thinking skills can be improved through broad training how many students can be expected to discover the processes of evolu-

34. *Ibid.*, p. 268.
35. David P. Ausubel, "Learning by Discovery: Rationale and Mystique," *National Association of Secondary School Principals*, December, 1961, p. 37.

tion, nuclear fission, or gravitation without carefully contrived arrangements which turn out to be just another means of transmitting new ideas and facts?

According to Bruner one of the benefits of discovery learning is that the child who learns to discover something rather than simply learning about something is likely to be free from the control of extrinsic motives, e.g., grades, or praise. However, Ausubel disagrees that discovery or reflective thinking has any necessary connection with intrinsic motivation for learning. He contends that individuals who learn for extrinsic motives are those who lack intrinsic self-esteem, hence they have a greater need for compensating their lack of self-esteem, with such symbols of achievement as high grades, teacher approval, and the prestige that comes with self-discovery. Put in another way, since American culture attaches a high premium on self-discovery, emphasis on problem solving and discovery is more likely to lead to learning for extrinsic rather than intrinsic motives. Beyond this, there is still another and more practical objection. That is, considering the present educational arrangements and the fact that society itself requires certain minimum proficiency in a number of specified disciplines within a limited time period, it is simply not practical to insist that every student must discover every concept and principle in various fields by himself. Indeed, such a demand would not make it possible for our students even at the university level to go much beyond the very elementary level of understanding in any discipline.

On the basis of these and other shortcomings we need not go into here, Ausubel suggests that the school "concentrate its major efforts on teaching both what is most important in terms of cultural survival and progress and what is most teachable to the majority of its clientele."[36] He further recommends that our teaching should be based on the principle of progressive differentiation and integrative reconcilia-

---

36. *Ibid.*, p. 41.

tion.[37] In other words, effective teaching should proceed by introducing organizers or certain fundamental concepts of a discipline around which new ideas, information, and principles are integrated and interrelated. These organizers should be presented in order of inclusiveness. For example, in biology we may first introduce the concept of life, then animals and plants, and so on. These organizers can be prepared according to individual disciplines as well as units of a discipline. An advantage of this approach to teaching is that by first presenting organizers the learner is given not only an overview of what he is to learn but also the elements which will help him integrate and interrelate newly learned material with the knowledge and experiences he already possesses.

Ausubel is correct in arguing that expository verbal teaching is not inherently meaningless and authoritarian, nor is reflective teaching necessarily effective and more desirable unless it is tautologically defined as "that form of teaching which is effective and meaningful." Certainly the pedagogic strategies which are contrived in such a way that students are *led to discover* certain predetermined concepts or principles or to "solve" problems according to a prescribed manner are as educationally barren as verbal teaching which concentrates on rote learning of unrelated facts. On the other hand, we have seen how reflective teaching fosters critical and creative thinking and encourages students to become autonomous learners. We have also witnessed the situations where expository verbal teaching proved to be effective in stimulating critical thinking and in integrating knowledge with experience. In all fairness to the proponents of reflective teaching it must be pointed out that reflective teaching is not defined as a set of specific steps guaranteed to produce desirable educational consequences. To be sure, reflective thinking does require certain indispensable elements, but these elements represent a logic of inquiry rather than steps or procedures to be followed by students. We must remember that the central concern of

37. David P. Ausubel, *Psychology of Meaningful Verbal Learning*, pp. 79–83.

reflective thinking is that teaching should result in integrated learning experiences which will enable the learner to deal with constant change and various problems in an increasingly effective and efficient way. The kind of teaching which leads to these consequences may require many different activities and procedures. In some areas of study expository verbal teaching may be more suitable than the problem-solving or inquiry method. In other areas problem solving or the discovery approach may be more appropriate. The teacher's decision to use the discovery or the expository approach should depend on the nature of the subject matter, the interest of the child, and his background and capacities, as well as on the availability of time, resource materials, and even physical facilities. The most vital aspect of reflective thinking is the kind of climate which will allow children to examine critically accepted beliefs, analyze new ideas, and propose imaginative solutions to problems. It is in this sense that self-discovery (or rediscovery) of knowledge is so important, because such an experience will permit a child to appreciate the world of scholars and scientists and also give him self-confidence, respect for his ability, as well as confidence in man's ability to cope with his perplexities intelligently. To attain this end,

> children need not discover all generalizations for themselves, obviously. Yet we want to give them opportunity to develop a decent competence at it and a proper confidence in their ability to operate independently. . . . For if we do nothing else, we should somehow give to children a respect for their own powers of thinking, for their power to generate good questions, to come up with interesting informed guesses.[38]

AN ALTERNATIVE: CONFLUENT EDUCATION

A considerably different criticism of reflective thinking comes from those who accuse our schools of having focused their attention exclusively on cognitive or intellectual learn-

38. Bruner, *Theory of Instruction*, p. 96.

ing. While these critics are not against discovery experience, they object to reflective teaching on the ground that imagination and the emotional or affective domain of the child's life are not sufficiently emphasized. Psychologists George Issac Brown and Richard M. Jones both argue that the kind of teaching which is predominantly concerned with cognitive learning is not adequate, because "there is no intellectual learning without some sort of feeling, and there are no feelings without the mind's being somehow involved."[39] Consequently, in their opinion a sound view of teaching should recognize and suggest the appropriate ways of guiding not only intellectually-oriented children but also those who are predisposed to feelings and fantasies.[40] If we emphasized the cognitive skills only and left the emotional and imaginative skills to random development we are likely to encourage pedantry in the intellectually-oriented child, anti-intellectualism in the emotionally predisposed child, and estrangement in those who are more fantasy oriented.[41] Therefore, children should be taught so that "the affective domain and the cognitive domain flow together, like two streams merging into one river, and are thus integrated in individual and group learning."[42] In brief, what is needed is confluent education.

Confluent education, which asks for coordination of the intellectual, the emotional, and the imaginative dimensions of the learner, stems from what is sometimes called the Third Force Psychology or phenomenological or existential psychology. The so-called phenomenological psychology is a form of introspectionism which seeks pure description of phenomenal experience, raw experience, or experience as given. It differs from the Tichenerean introspectionism we discussed earlier (see "Structural Psychology" in Chapter 3) in that human experience is *not* seen as being divisible into certain elementary sensations. Phenomenologists deny that

39. George Issac Brown, *Human Teaching for Human Learning*, p. 4.
40. Richard M. Jones, *Fantasy and Feeling in Education*, p. 197.
41. *Ibid.*, p. 198.
42. Brown, *Human Teaching*, p. 19.

man's experience is reducible to sense data, hence raw or unanalyzed experience becomes the basis of psychological science. And since private experiences as they occur to the person are at the base of phenomenological terms, they are not publicly verifiable. But if scientific knowledge depends upon communication of reports of individual experiences and their intersubjective verification, how can such private experiences be useful in psychology? According to Abraham Maslow, a humanistic psychologist, the conventional method of public verification is not possible in phenomenology, but communication of private experience is possible "through intimacy to the mystical fusion in which the two people become one in a phenomenological way."[43] In other words, we can know about another man's experience by becoming the other. We know it because we know ourselves and this knowledge becomes a part of us. Thus we gain experiential knowledge, which is the best kind of knowledge for human purposes. Hence, the best way to know about something is to move toward fusion with it. To move toward fusion with anyone is to care for him or even love him. And a law of learning and cognizing is caring.[44] To love the object to be known is to be interested in it, for it is difficult to do anything about the object which totally bores us. Accordingly the fruitful inquirer "is the one who talks about his 'problem' in about the same spirit as he does about the woman he loves, as an end rather than as a means to other ends."[45] In this way the person becomes completely undivided in his attention and totally devoted to his work.

One of the main premises underlying phenomenology is the assumption that each man has an inner nature which is either good or neutral and it is in part unique to the individual and in part species-wide. This nature is not only knowable scientifically, but when we allow it to grow and develop and also have it guide our life, we become happy, healthy, and fruitful. On

43. Abraham H. Maslow, *The Psychology of Science*, p. 103.
44. *Ibid.*, p. 104.
45. *Ibid.*, p. 110.

the other hand, suppression or ignoring of the inner nature makes us sick. This means the more we know about a man's inner tendencies the easier it will be to show him how he can become happy, healthy and productive, and also gain self-respect and achieve the maximum realization of his capacities. We must then find out what the other person is really like inside as a member of human society and as a particular individual. Such a view of man's nature calls for the kind of education which will place its major emphasis on the development of man's potentiality to be human, understanding himself and others, and achieving human needs and self-actualization. Thus, sound education would require that we cultivate self-discipline, spontaneity, and creativity all at the same time and that classroom teaching be related to life situations.

THE ROLE OF TEACHING

"Teaching is, for me, a relatively unimportant and vastly over-valued activity.[46] These are the words of Carl R. Rogers, one of the most influential phenomenological psychologists, who is convinced that it is not possible for a person to teach anything to anyone. Hence, he thinks that teaching is a matter of facilitating conditions for self-discovered learning.

> Self-discovered learning, truth that has been personally appropriated and assimilated in experience, cannot be directly communicated to another. As soon as an individual tries to communicate such experience directly, often with a quite natural enthusiasm, it becomes teaching, and its results are inconsequential.[47]

But what are the necessary conditions for learning and what must the teacher do to facilitate such conditions? According to Rogers, human beings have a natural potentiality for learning in that they are curious about their world. This

46. Carl R. Rogers, *Interpersonal Relationships in the Facilitation of Learning*, p. 2.
47. Carl R. Rogers, *On Becoming a Person*, p. 276.

curiosity or desire to know develops until they are smothered by their experiences in our schools. Thus we must remove restrictions and the suppressive climate of the learning environment and cultivate this natural capacity for learning. One of the main reasons why the suppressive and punitive climate of the learning situation must be eliminated is that the child resists any experience which threatens the self. We need to provide the child with a more supportive, understanding and nonthreatening environment for self-discovered learning. For example, a child who is having serious difficulty in reading should not be forced to recite or read aloud in front of his peers, whose reactions may often reinforce the child's own perception of himself as a failure. Rogers believes that significant learning is promoted by allowing children to confront directly various problematic situations, whether they are social, ethical, philosophical, or practical. And by having the learner choose his own directions, discover his own resources, formulate his own problems, decide his own course of action, and accept the consequences of his choice, significant learning can be maximized. In sum, significant learning is difficult to achieve unless the feelings as well as the intellect of the child are involved, and if a child is to be educated to become a self-reliant, creative, and independent person he must be given opportunities to evaluate and criticize his own efforts, successes as well as mistakes.

Now, since these are conditions under which Rogers believes meaningful learning can occur, the teacher's primary responsibility is to facilitate them by (1) setting the initial mood of the group, (2) helping to clarify the purposes of the individuals as well as the group itself, (3) organizing and making available the widest range of resources, (4) regarding himself as a flexible resource to be used by the group, (5) taking the initiative in sharing his feelings and thoughts with the group, and (6) remaining sensitive to the expression of deep or strong feelings by the individual students.[48] In the

48. Carl R. Rogers, *Freedom to Learn*, pp. 164–166.

process of functioning as the facilitator of these learning conditions the teacher, too, becomes a participating learner, and he must maintain certain essential attitudes toward his students. Rogers advises us that an effective teacher must be real or genuine to his students, while prizing or accepting the learner.[49] He must also have empathic understanding of his pupils. In brief, to be genuine is not to enter into a relationship with the learner by presenting a front, but to meet the learner on a person-to-person basis, i.e., to be oneself. In this way the teacher can accept his feelings as his own, and therefore he will have no need to impose them on his students. Consequently, "he can like or dislike a student product without implying that it is objectively good or bad or that the student is good or bad."[50] The second essential attitude, prizing the student's feelings, opinions, and his person, is the same as caring for the learner, who has worth in his own right. This is a nonpossessive caring (some call it nonpossessive warmth) based on the assumption that the learner is trustworthy. Thus the teacher accepts him as an imperfect being with many feelings and potentialities. Empathic understanding is the third attitude which establishes a climate for self-initiated learning. That is, when the teacher is able to understand his students' reactions, predicaments, and aspirations by placing himself in the learner's place the likelihood of significant learning is also increased. Empathic understanding is not a form of evaluative understanding, which involves making judgments about the other person as being good or bad, efficient or inefficient, and so on. Empathic understanding has to do with seeing things as the other person sees them himself without making any evaluation or analysis. Hence, the learner is likely to say "Now I can blossom and grow and learn," because he is free from imposition and the fear of disapproval.[51] In facilitating all of these conditions and attitudes for

---

49. Rogers, *Interpersonal Relationships*, pp. 6–14. Three attitudes are discussed.
50. *Ibid.*, p. 6.
51. *Ibid.*, p. 13.

self-initiated learning, the teacher must always remember that whatever the child learns must be relevant to him, and that this relevance is determined by the learner's perception of the relationship between what he is to learn and his personal purposes. As Brown puts it, we know something is relevant "when it is personally meaningful, when we have feelings about it."[52] In other words, if a child does not *feel* that having a certain knowledge and skill is relevant in achieving a particular goal such knowledge and skill are not relevant. Thus, significant learning is said to take place when the subject matter is seen by the learner as relevant to his own purpose.[53]

REFLECTIVE TEACHING AND THE PHENOMENOLOGICAL CONCEPT

A comparison of reflective teaching with the Rogerean concept of teaching shows that both stress the importance of self-discovery and relating learning experiences to the child's life. But the reflective view appears to emphasize the cognitive or the intellectual aspect of learning more than the affective domain. This seeming imbalance may be accounted for by the fact that the proponents of reflective thinking see the emotional elements of the child's intellectual processes as an inseparable part of the entire context of the teaching-learning situation. Hence, reflective teaching does not consist only of specific steps to be followed by the learner but it also and necessarily includes certain attitudes and interpersonal relationships. Reflective teaching aims at helping the learner attain new insights, imaginative solutions to problems, and confidence in his ability to deal with various indeterminate situations, but the kinds of learning experiences which are likely to lead to these educational consequences cannot occur in an environment which is authoritarian, suppressive, and

52. Brown, *Human Teaching*, p. 10.
53. Rogers, *Freedom to Learn*, p. 149.

punitive. This suggests that the learner's own perceptions, thoughts, and interests are important in effective teaching. It does *not* imply that the learner's subjective feeling is the only criterion of relevance, for there are many circumstances in which actions based solely on the person's feelings lead to some disastrous consequences. The concept of relevance implies a means-ends connection. That is, we say that an idea or a way of acting is relevant when it helps us achieve a particular purpose. Implicit in this interpretation of relevance is the belief that some objective knowledge and certain specialized skills are essential if we hope to be successful in realizing our goals. We cannot "split" an atom with a hammer regardless of how we *feel* about it. The splitting of an atom necessarily requires objective knowledge, which can be transmitted and developed by many different means. On the other hand, if what is known as relevant is to be utilized in accomplishing an objective it is necessary that the person see the connection between certain means and ends. In short, the notion of relevance has both subjective and objective dimensions and in a very real sense it would be immoral and certainly unprofessional for a teacher to permit a child to do something which he knows to be harmful on objective grounds just because the child *feels* like doing it.

Criticism of Phenomenology

In regard to the nature of self-discovered knowledge, Rogers is correct in claiming that self-discovered knowledge cannot be directly communicated to another person, if he means that we cannot completely comprehend (or apprehend) the content and the meaning of another person's experience. Of course, complete understanding of another man's ideas or experiences is impossible, for we cannot think, reason, imagine, and feel as others do. We can only approximate both the cognitive and affective dimensions of another individual's life. Yet, we do in fact communicate much of what we know and experience either by direct expression or by the use of such indirect vehicles as music, poetry, painting, etc. There is no reason why the teacher cannot utilize these same means in an imaginative way to communicate his ideas, experiences, and even feelings. All experiences have subjective elements, simply because it is the person himself who undergoes them. But to become preoccupied with the personal aspects of experience alone is to make all thoughts and feelings completely inaccessible to others.

In stressing the impossibility of directly communicating self-discovered truth, Rogers indicated that he found some solace in learning that Søren Kierkegaard shared the same belief.[54] But it appears that Rogers misunderstood Kierkegaard's primary concern. In his book *Concluding Unscientific Postscript* Kierkegaard held that truth was subjective and that indirect rather than direct vehicles are better suited for communicating such truth. However, for Kierkegaard the term *truth* did not represent a quality of judgment or a proposition (scientific *truth, true* knowledge, etc.), but rather it stood for a quality belonging to the relationship between a man and his beliefs. Thus when an individual acts according to his beliefs in spite of possible danger he is said to be in the truth.[55] In this context truth as a belief means the essential truth or the principle by which a man is willing to live and die. Kierkegaard did not insist that self-discovered truth of any kind cannot be communicated to others. As a matter of fact, in his *Journals* he indicated that objective knowledge is not only possible but its understanding is necessary in so far as it must precede our action. What Kierkegaard did reject was the claim that objective knowledge or a rational system, whether philosophical or scientific, can explain each man's existential predicaments. Now, returning to Roger's position, what children discover in their learning experiences is not limited to the so-called essential truths, for they can and do discover truths as related to various fields of knowledge. Therefore, unless

54. Rogers, *On Becoming a Person*, p. 276.
55. Søren Kierkegaard, *Concluding Unscientific Postscript*, D. F. Swenson and Walter Lowrie, trans. Truth as Subjectivity is discussed in pp. 178–183.

we are careful in making distinctions between the existential or essential truth and epistemological truths we mislead our students and their teachers into thinking that all knowledge is a matter of subjective judgement based on feelings and preferences. Indeed, this belief does not make the child become an autonomous learner, rather it makes him capricious and irresponsible.

One of the perplexing aspects of Rogers' view of teaching is the language he uses to describe certain variables which are said to affect the child's learning experiences. As was discussed earlier, Rogers indicated three attitudes as important variables influencing the outcome of the child's learning process. They were *genuineness, prizing,* and *empathy.* There is little doubt that these terms will elicit many different feelings in various individuals. But Rogers did not give a clear idea of the things we must do to become genuine, prizing, and empathic, for his explanations consist of a series of terms which remain ambiguous and vague. For example, he explained *genuineness* as identical with *realness,* which in turn was synonymous with accepting the child on a person-to-person basis, and so on. If we are to become effective facilitators of learning conditions in Rogers' sense, at some point in his explanation he must eventually point to an act or a series of acts, and/or a condition or a complex of conditions.

Rogers' claim that we can express our feelings about the learner's work without making any evaluative judgment is a rather strange suggestion. Emotions and the intellect are not separable as the proponents of confluent education claim. How can we say, "I don't like your work. But that's just my feeling, not my evaluation"? If Rogers is suggesting that in evaluating the work of our students we should not make moral judgments about their character, he is saying something quite obvious. But in a teaching-learning situation the most helpful kind of judgment is the one that contains evaluative elements. That is, it is more helpful to say, "I don't like your work, because it does not clearly express your ideas," and so on.

THE FIELD THEORY OF BEHAVIOR

Of all the theories of human behavior and learning we have examined in this book, Lewin's field theory appears to be the most adequate and sound approach to the study of man, his behavior, his society and their interrelationships, because it attempts to give us a comprehensive theoretical framework, which can account for the behavior of individuals as well as behavior in general. Furthermore, the field theory also gives us a scheme by which we can scientifically deal with those aspects of man's mental processes which cannot be satisfactorily described or explained in terms of discrete overt responses alone. In other words, rather than dismissing all mentalistic terms as fictions Lewin attempts to provide an objective means by which such mentalistic processes and states as motivation, tension, need, expectancy, and so on can be explained, predicted, and better controlled. In short, the field theory can account for our subjective experiences and perceptions as well as the objective observation of external events. However, some critics argue that since man often acts because of his past history or anticipated future, Lewin's premise that human behavior is caused only by the present condition of the cognitive structure, life space, is only partially valid. In other words, by stressing the contemporaneity of life space the Lewineans have ruled out the possibility of the past or the future playing any significant role in psychology and human behavior. Indeed, neither past nor future events can cause a present response, because they do not exist as events here and now. Yet our *memory* of the past and *anticipation* of the future have psychological forces which influence our behavior. What matters is not that past and future events must exist as events now, but that they belong to the individual's psychological world. As Lewin puts it: "The existence or nonexistence and the time index of a psychological fact are independent of the existence or nonexistence and time index of the fact to which its content refers."[56] A related but a more serious objection to the principle of contemporaneity is that by insisting a person's behavior cannot be influenced by a force which is not within the individual's consciousness the field theorists ignore the fact that the culture and social structure of a society affect human behavior independently of the individual's perception of it because, "a person's perceptions are a function not only of his [the individual's] sensitivities but also of the available stimuli, many of them derived from culture and social structure."[57] This is an astute observation and as field theorists we need not disagree with it, for field theory does not assert that perception is purely a biological or a physical process. On the contrary, the way in which a person perceives ideas and objects and the meanings he assigns to them contain certain elements of the socio-cultural structure in which he lives. The nature of the individual and the structure of his life space are not separable from the culture and social structure of his society.

THE FUNCTIONAL CONCEPT OF MIND

The functional concept of mind is the result of an attempt to give a naturalistic account of man and his mind without engaging in metaphysical speculations. Hence, it is consistent with both personal experience and the findings of modern science. The notion that man's mind is his ability to respond to present stimuli by anticipating the future consequences is based on the premise that both life and mind are functions of organisms and that neither could exist apart from a neurophysiological structure of some kind. This means the mind does not exist as either a material or non material entity, because it is a function of the total organism in exactly the same sense in which motion is a function of bodies or the expenditure of

56. Kurt Lewin, *Principles of Topological Psychology*, Fritz Heider, trans., p. 39.
57. Milton J. Yinger, "Research Implications of a Field View of Personality," *American Journal of Sociology*, Vol. 68, No. 5, March 1963, p. 583.

energy. Motion, of course, is not a mysterious entity and neither is the mind. Hence, functionalists maintain that mental processes presuppose neurophysiological processes within the brain and the nervous system. But they deny that what is mental can be reduced to the physical. In other words, mentalistic terms represent something more than a layman's way of talking about complex neural processes. And consequently, statements about mental experiences cannot be completely translated into pure physicalistic propositions. For example, the term *lightning* is identical with the statement "an exchange of electric charges between two layers of ionized cloud." But "I see lightning" is not identical with either "an exchange of electric charges between two layers of ionized cloud" or another physicalistic description of a person ("I") seeing lightning. The concept "I" in the sense of self-consciousness cannot be translated into a statement containing only those terms which we use to describe objects. Even in psychological terms, "*I* am hungry" is not equivalent to deprivation of food.

Implicit in the functional concept of mind is the premise that mind is a development of matter. In other words, as functionalists we may assert that reality is physical and that this physical reality has many different aspects functioning in varied ways. Since there are different functions of matter, different languages are needed to describe such functions. In other words, our mental processes are physical processes but they are radically different from physical processes in the usual sense. The reason mentalistic terms cannot be completely translated into physicalistic terms is because mentalistic language is the most appropriate language for describing certain complex physical events which we call mental events. The mental and the physical can be distinguished from each other not as separate entities but only as vastly different aspects of a single reality, which is physical. In this way we can insist that the mind is man's ability to solve problems, or to order means to certain ends in view, or his ability to act purposively with a plan for the future, without denying that all of these are manifestations, in the broadest sense, of complex physical processes.

BIBLIOGRAPHY

Books

Aune, Bruce, *Knowledge, Man, and Nature.* New York: Random House, 1967.

Ausubel, David P., *Psychology of Meaningful Verbal Learning.* New York: Grune and Straton, 1963.

———— "Some Psychological and Educational Limitations of Learning by Discovery," *Readings in School Learning,* David P. Ausubel, ed. New York: Holt, Rinehart and Winston, 1969.

Brown, George Issac, *Human Teaching for Human Learning.* New York: The Viking Press, 1971.

Bruner, Jerome S., "Needed: A Theory of Instruction," *Contemporary Thought on Teaching,* Ronald T. Hyman, ed. Englewood Cliffs, N.J.: Prentice-Hall, Inc., 1971.

———— *On Knowing.* New York: Atheneum, 1967.

———— *The Process of Education.* Cambridge: Harvard University Press, 1963.

———— *Toward a Theory of Instruction.* Cambridge: Harvard University Press, 1966.

Dewey, John, *Democracy and Education.* New York: The Macmillan Co., 1916.

———— *How We Think.* Boston: D. C. Heath & Co., 1933.

Hullfish, Gordon H., and Philip G. Smith, *Reflective Thinking.* New York: Dodd, Mead & Co., 1961.

Jones, Richard M., *Fantasy and Feeling in Education.* New York: New York University Press, 1968.

Kierkegaard, Søren, *Concluding Unscientific Postscript,* D. F. Swenson, and W. Lowrie, trans. Princeton: Princeton University Press, 1941.

Lewin, Kurt, *Field Theory in Social Science,* Dorwing Cartwright, ed. New York: Harper and Row, 1951.

—— *Principles of Topological Psychology*, Fritz Heider, trans. New York: McGraw-Hill Book Co., Inc., 1936.

Maslow, Abraham H., *The Psychology of Science.* Chicago: Henry Regnery Co., 1966.

Mead, George H., *Mind, Self, and Society.* Chicago: University of Chicago Press, 1934.

—— *The Philosophy of the Present.* Chicago: Open Court Publishing Co., 1932.

Postman, Neil, and Charles Weingartner, *Teaching as a Subversive Activity.* New York: Delacorte Press, 1969.

Rogers, Carl R., *Freedom to Learn.* Columbus, Ohio: Charles E. Merrill Publishing Co., 1969.

—— *On Becoming a Person.* Boston: Houghton Mifflin Co., 1961.

—— *Interpersonal Relationships in the Facilitation of Learning.* Columbus, Ohio: Charles E. Merrill Publishing Co., 1961.

Periodicals

Ausubel, David P. "Learning by Discovery: Rationale and Mystique." *National Association of Secondary School Principals*, Dec., 1961.

Yinger, J. Milton "Research Implications of a Field View of Personality." *American Journal of Sociology*, Vol. 68, No. 5, March 1963.

INDEX